I KNOW YOU'RE GOING TO BE HAPPY

I KNOW YOU'RE GOING TO BE HAPPY

A Story of Love and Betrayal

RUPERT CHRISTIANSEN

Published in 2013 by Short Books

3A Exmouth House
Pine Street
EC1R 0JH

10 9 8 7 6 5 4 3 2 1

A CIP catalogue record for this book
is available from the British Library.

ISBN 978-1-78072-124-8

Printed in Great Britain by CPI Group (UK) Ltd.
Croydon, CR0 4YY

for Ellis Woodman

On Sunday mornings my father would briefly play at being Daddy.

He worked so hard through such long and late shifts in Fleet Street that I seldom saw him otherwise, and when I left for nursery school in the morning he was invariably still supine in bed, a snoring heap of striped pyjama. In an attempt to rouse him, my mother once announced: 'There's a French onion seller in the lavatory' – and she wasn't joking. In the 1950s, such figures were commonly seen cycling around the suburbs and this poor fellow had knocked at the door, pleading so piteously for permission to relieve himself that my mother had ushered him in. But my father just snored on, oblivious or uncaring.

On Sunday mornings, things were different. Being chief sub-editor on a Sunday newspaper, he could afford to relax a little once the Saturday evening deadline had been met. After breakfast, we would walk together down to the local newsagent – in those days, virtually the only retail life permitted on the Sabbath – and he would give me a silver sixpenny piece and allow me to select my own menu of cheap sweets: four for a penny Trebor Chews, a sherbet fountain (sucked through a liquorice straw), a tube of Love Hearts, that sort of thing. I was four or five and while I know I enjoyed these ritual outings – not least from the sugar-rush angle – the only specific memory they have left is the one which follows.

A photographer from my office is coming to tea this afternoon, he said. He is going to take pictures of us all – you, me, Mummy, and Anna the baby too. Act naturally and don't play up to the camera, he said, and I wondered what this injunction might imply. This is a weirdly vivid but isolated memory.

So the photographer arrived. He seemed nice. He sat on a chair by the window in the sitting room. He used a big camera with a frightening, excitingly explosive flashlight attached. Chocolate biscuits were on offer, a treat, served on the best Rockingham bone china. Click, click-click, click. The photographs were taken, and I have prints of them still.

They look professional, certainly a cut above the average family snap. My father is cross-legged on the floor playing with my sister and me. My mother sits apart doling out the tea, looking tense and wary. I am giving rein to my ingrained histrionic streak by trying hard to act naturally, while Anna is just an enchantingly plump and restless baby smudged with milk and Farex. I note now some of the period details: my teddy bear, the jazzy Festival of Britain wallpaper and Ercol furniture, the good wool carpet. The television is on: the Sunday afternoon classic serial, of which there will be more to say.

But do not suppose that this domestic tableau is innocent. These photographs were being taken for an urgent reason, as if to bear witness to an event that would be momentous in all our lives. Many years later, my mother told me that this was the day that my father had told her that their eleven-year marriage was over. He could only explain that hard though he had tried, he could not be the person she wanted him to be. He had fallen in love with his secretary and he had chosen to spend the rest of his life with her. He was leaving now, irrevocably and permanently, and he had commissioned the photographs so that he could take away something through which to remember us.

My mother claimed later that she had had no wind of this. In shock, she at first assumed that he was mad or joking – which given his raffish, impulsive eccentricity would not have been altogether out of character. But he wasn't playing a game, or having a brainstorm, or hedging his bets: he had rationally decided to go for good, leaving not only his wife but a four-year-old son and seven-month-old daughter as well. A betrayal that must have lacerated his conscience for the rest of his life, you might think. That is as far as my memory of the day extends

— I can't pretend to recall a tearful farewell or a door slamming. There is one other thing — one other quite extraordinary thing, relating to the television serial — but I shall leave that for later, when you know more about us.

———————

The past can be every bit as terrifying as the future, a maze of unquiet ghosts and the shocks of memory, pitted with dark corners, unexpected turnings and locked doors. My mother felt this keenly: she was full of remorse but without nostalgia. So when I went through her papers after she died in 2004, it didn't surprise me to realise that she had covered her tracks quite carefully, throwing away photographs and documents and destroying almost all her correspondence.

But that 'almost' pulls me up short: why and how did the odd item survive? I wonder, for example, whether the letter that follows slipped through the cull by accident or design. It was sent by a senior Fleet Street figure to my parents, both up-and-coming young journalists on the *Daily Mail*, before their wedding in 1948. Did my mother keep it from the bonfire in a spirit of grim irony? Or did she intend that my sister or I might one day find it and understand that she and my father had set out on their life together in a spirit of love and hope?

My dear Michael and my dear Kathleen,

You don't know how sorry I am that I can't be in at the kill, so to speak, on Saturday. Partly because I love a Fleet Street occasion, but more particularly, because I love you both, and wanted to see your happiness together.

Now Fleet Street romances are supposed to be very risky affairs, foredoomed to difficulties and troubles that other young married couples don't have. I do not believe a word of it. I think that two people, sharing the common interest of journalism, our beloved trade, and especially being good reporters, means a very big asset to start off with.

So with your shared journalistic love, your youth and your love for each other, you just can't miss.

I know you're going to be happy, and you will be very much in my thoughts on Saturday.

God bless you both.

'I know you're going to be happy' was a remark that fate would find too tempting. They were not blessed and they did miss, as journalism, their 'beloved trade', turned from friend to enemy, and their marriage turned into a divorce which, as Tolstoy put it, in another context, was 'most simple and most ordinary and therefore most terrible'.

The ancient Greek myth of Medea – dramatised by Euripides, composed by Cherubini, painted by Delacroix, filmed by Pasolini – is a template of divorce. I can't think of anything else that presents so intensely the self-harming nature of the emotions involved: the necrotic remorse, the vortex of blame, the ricochet of accusations, the boiling cauldron of rage at the waste of love. How could I be such a blind fool, how could I have sold myself so short as to surrender so much to anyone as worthless, as ignoble, as faithless, as weak as you? And how do I get even?

Medea, a princess of the outpost of Colchis, falls in love with the marauding Greek hero Jason. Using her magic powers, she helps him steal the treasure of the Golden Fleece, to which he has no birthright. In becoming his wife and mother to his sons, she leaves her homeland, deserts her family and enrages her gods. Transported to the alien civilisation of Corinth, Jason abandons her and decides to marry Glauce, a young woman of his own race and social status, younger, fresher, more biddable and blind to his failings. Medea is humiliatingly sent to live outside the city walls. Jason tells her that he means her no harm. He holds her in respect and wishes her happiness, it's just that ... one's feelings change ...

and there's nothing one can do about it ...

She will not listen and tempers explode. He demands custody of the children. She refuses and he storms out. He thinks she is insane, she thinks he is a swine. Licking her wounds, she hatches a plan, a dastardly but brilliant plan which won't see her triumph so much as drag him down to an anguish worse than hers. Pretending to have relented and acknowledged her fault, she sends Glauce a peace offering in the form of an intricately woven and exquisitely bejewelled wedding dress. But its lining is coated with a venomous potion which will flay and scald her the moment she wears it. How Medea gloats as she imagines Glauce's screams and the way that, crazed with the searing pain, she will leap from the city walls to her death.

That's not all. Jason wants the children, but they are hers, entirely hers – the fruit of her womb, so dearly loved and nurtured and prized that nobody else, not even their idiot father, can lay claim to them. There is only one impregnable way to ensure her total possession: she must kill them, thus at one stroke both keeping them hers for ever and causing Jason further unimaginable grief. The fact that it will leave her entirely desolate too can't be helped, and in any case what does it matter, what does she care? Jason has already eviscerated her.

No, of course, it isn't always quite as bad as that,

though as I read in the newspapers today of the scorned, scornful (and Greek) Vicky Pryce, ex-wife to the Liberal Democrat minister Chris Huhne, I cannot but think of Medea. Today, there are divorces through which everyone behaves frightfully well and stays friends and attends each other's subsequent weddings – where Jason and Medea peck each other's cheeks as the kids are dropped off, where Medea and Glauce end up on girly shopping expeditions, giggling about Jason's little willy over their lattes. Divorce is a social norm now, and can even be treated as a bit of a joke: people have parties to celebrate the split and gaily auction off their chattels. More soberly, there are divorces which generate a feeling of relief and liberation, and those which are solidly and rationally forged out of mutual consent.

But not very many, and even fewer before the concept of blame was removed from the statute books in 1969 – a reform which my mother fiercely and bitterly opposed. Imagine 1960, when my parents began 'proceedings', and you are in a culture in which the divorce courts are gladiatorial arenas where two goaded, stuck wild beasts can barely be restrained from tearing each other to pieces in ritual combat. It isn't my fault; he started it, she started it. It's not about the cash, or even access to the children: ultimately, it is about honour. Divorce is revenge, nothing less, and blood money is at stake.

1.

Let me start with my father. He is a mystery to me: after the age of five, I never saw him again. From him I have inherited half my genes and at least some of my personality traits, but I can only guess what these might be, and if I start looking into my self, I soon encounter shadows moving anonymously speaking words that I cannot quite hear: this must be him, but there is no way that I can penetrate the scrim.

A very few stray mental snapshots and ungrounded incidents such as the photographer's tea party aside, I cannot remember him. I often thought, even as a child, that if I passed him in the street, I would not recognise him. I can't recall his voice and I have only ever seen one photograph of him looking older than about 30 – a portrait by David Bailey, piquantly enough, which I encountered by chance when I was at a friend's house, casually flicking through a book recording 'iconic' figures of the 1960s called *Goodbye*

Baby and Amen. I saw the face before I registered the caption, and thought it looked vaguely familiar. So that's where I got my piggy ski-jump nose, my Viking square head and brow, my thin lips and watchful gaze.

My grandfather was marked by these features too. He will be a crucial if largely absent figure in this narrative, and although he had no malign intentions, he has a lot to answer for. His name was Arthur Christiansen, and in his day he was widely famous as the editor of the *Daily Express*, a newspaper owned by Lord Beaverbrook, which under my grandfather's leadership revolutionised popular journalism and coasted on a daily circulation of over four million copies: he would, incidentally, have been appalled at the depths to which it has sunk today, not to mention the long, slow, painful decline of the entire industry.

His credo was to 'remember the people in the back streets of Derby' and that 'every word that appeared in at any rate my newspaper must be clear and comprehensible to them. Must be interesting to them, must encourage them to break away from littleness, stimulate their ambition, help them to want to build a better land.' Under this banner, the *Express* became a byword for sharp, fresh reportage, pitched in lucid and incisive prose. He may have been accused of allowing the paper to become the mouthpiece for his proprietor's personal agenda – anti-Wallis Simpson, pro-Churchill and generally conservative – and his obsequious letters to Beaverbrook in the archives suggest that this was not a baseless slur. But there was never any doubt of his extraordinary ability to put an attractive newspaper together, underpinned by a genius for projecting and communicating news.

'Chris', as he was widely and affectionately known (and as I shall refer to him), was not only a superb technician, with an infallible instinct for the prioritising of stories and striking visual layouts, but also a popular and inspiring boss who led from the front. He could spot talent a mile off and knew how to coax the best out of his journalists, often massaging their necks while they sweated to meet a deadline. 'I praise when I can and kick when I have to,' he said. His daily bulletins, posted in the office to review the previous day's paper, became legendary and his lapidary injunctions, such as:

There is often a lot of news to be got out of shop windows.

It is the journalistic fashion to concentrate on the first paragraphs of stories. I believe in that. But I believe just as emphatically in the perfection of the last paragraph.

You cannot beat news in a newspaper.

are still quoted today.

Chris was not the product of privilege. Born in 1904 into the lower-middle-class suburb of Wallasey, his parents were a working-class English mother and a Danish father, whose own father had emigrated to Liverpool to work as a shipwright. As far as I can research, there was nothing remarkable about the family on either side, beyond a Danish aunt who married into the Carlsberg beer dynasty and was said to have had published a couple of children's books (of which I can find no record in any library catalogue).

Chris was a bright lad who left grammar school burning with ambition, and almost at once made a splash on a local rag. He came south to London at the age of twenty, where he thought 'journalists were gods who walked on air' and Fleet Street a place 'of dreaming spires'. Soon he got a job on the *Sunday Express* and then made his name when as night editor he scooped the R101 airship disaster. Beaverbrook made him editor of the *Daily Express* in 1933 at a princely salary of £5,000 per annum and he remained in the job until 1957, when he suffered a heart attack and was rather brutally kicked out.

Subsequently, he worked as a consultant on several newspaper-related programmes for the newly established ATV, wrote his autobiography

Headlines All My Life, appeared as the subject of an episode of Eamonn Andrews' television show *This Is Your Life* and, most bizarrely, played himself in *The Day the Earth Caught Fire*, a sci-fi film about the end of the world directed by his friend Val Guest. His is possibly the most wooden and inept performance in cinema history. (I have never been able to track down Guest's next picture *80,000 Suspects*, in which he took another cameo role as Mr Graney, editor of the *Bath Evening Chronicle*, a demoted guise in which I suspect his histrionic skills might show up even worse).

All this sounds like fun. Yet even though he was liberated from the killing pressure of producing a daily newspaper, his health worsened steadily through what would now be identified as 'stress-related' illnesses and he died suddenly from a thrombosis in 1963 at the age of 59. After his death, his wife Brenda wrote to thank Beaverbrook for his condolences. 'There is really only one thing to say to you,' she wrote cheekily. 'You have lost a son who loved you so much.'

In *Headlines All My Life* he had written: 'Newspaper wives are much to be pitied: they are in many ways more lonely and frustrated than the wives of sailors. A sailor's wife at least knows when her husband's ship is in port, but a newspaperman's wife rarely has any idea where her husband is.' Fortunately, Brenda, an aspiring actress from vaguely disreputable South London music-hall stock, didn't seem to mind his absence much: she had a thick hide and a taste for creature comforts that he could easily satisfy.

I don't think she was unhappy, but she had reason to feel uneasy: she couldn't have known what she was marrying and once Chris had rocketed to the top, she felt uncomfortable playing the subsidiary role of a sophisticated society hostess to which she was manifestly unsuited: this, at least, would explain both her affectations and heavy drinking. She caked herself in Helena Rubinstein and wore clunking gold jewellery and always struck me as selfish, trivial and a show-off. I thoroughly disliked her and as she was someone constantly on the verge of irritation or boredom or both, she scared me too: a lovable old granny she was not.

There were four children of this marriage – Michael, my father, born in 1927, Antoinette in 1931 and the twins Greta and Andrew in 1933 – and despite my grandfather's eighteen-hour days in Fleet Street (he kept a townhouse in nearby Westminster), cheerful and relatively normal family life flourished in a rambling mansion of no great architectural note called Little Holland Hall, near Frinton on the Essex coast. Here the main rooms had been showily deco-rated in the Syrie Maugham manner – a lot of white and beige, with quilted pink satin and silk upholstery – while the rest of the house remained penitentially dank and boarding-school drab.

Boisterous house parties filled the place at week-ends, fuelled by steady boozing (one of my earliest childhood memories is of the squish of the drawing-room soda siphon filling someone's crystal tumbler of whisky) and feasting. Those in attendance were more likely to be film than Fleet Street people, with Googie Withers and Alfred Hitchcock and his wife Alma held in special reverence. I get the sense that it was all a bit messy and sloppy and perhaps not very far from the world that Evelyn Waugh was satirising. But what did that matter? There were chauffeurs, nannies, housekeepers and skivvies on hand to do the hard work and clear up afterwards.

To me as a little boy Chris was known by the baby-name of Poodah, and noted for a Poodah kiss – a commodity he administered on the cheek not as the usual crisp, quick peck but as a sort of wet-fart smacker which made me laugh. As this may indicate, Chris was not without warmth or humanity: in fact, I believe he was pretty good fun, and I certainly know nothing dishonourable of him. But there was an unhealthy sense that his word was law. He had only to enter a room for the mood and pace to change. Nobody else got a look in. As the only success story in the extended family, his wealth was the lambent flame around which fluttered a lot of mothy distant relations, all keen to absorb whatever bounty he fitfully exuded. There wasn't an equitable balance of achievement, intelligence or labour in Little Holland Hall: it was the palace of an absolute monarch, entirely deferential to *un roi soleil* who answered only to God, aka Lord Beaverbrook.

Although *Headlines All My Life* discreetly provides scarcely any details of Chris's home life, my father makes a brief and touching appearance at the age of nine or ten, when he would be called upon to read the leader columns in the *Express*'s rival newspapers to Chris while he was soaking in his morning bath. Afterwards my father would scurry off to find a dictionary and look up the meaning of words that he had not understood, with the result that he soon developed a precocious literary style. The intimacy of this daily ritual suggests that my father adored his father with something akin to a hero-worship that would ultimately hobble him. He too wanted to be a great national newspaper editor and as he once told my mother in a manic-depressive frenzy, if he did not reach that goal by the time he was 40, he would simply kill himself. I don't think that this was an empty threat.

At the outbreak of war Chris, I have been told, was having an affair. He was also on Hitler's blacklist. However these factors weighed upon him relatively, he thought it wise to evacuate his family while a Nazi invasion seemed a genuine possibility. So Brenda and her four children left for the USA in July 1940, sailing on the *Washington*, the last boat that the Nazis permitted safe passage from the west coast of Ireland across the Atlantic, on the grounds that it contained neutral American civilians returning home.

But alongside them a few hundred wealthy Brits with connections and cash managed to swing their offspring on board too, and when the liner docked in Manhattan, the *New York Times* devoted nearly a whole page to the celebrity passenger list – including photographs of two Mountbatten girls off to lodge with the Vanderbilts and John Julius, son of the minister of information Duff Cooper and his celebrated wife Lady Diana, as well as Mrs Arthur Christiansen, wife of the editor of the London *Daily Express*, descending the gangplank with her brood of four. My father, geeky in a dark suit aged thirteen, towers lankily over his mother, who smiles for the camera. 'They will stay here with Mr and Mrs CV Thompson of Pound Ridge, NY,' the report stated. 'Mr Thompson is New York correspondent of the *Express* and Mrs Thompson is Dixie Tighe, a columnist on the *New York Post*.'

Much has been written about evacuees and the privations they suffered: I don't know whether my father and his siblings wanted to leave home, but they got off lightly, to say the least, landing up with their mother in an environment even more comfortable than the one they had left. Pound Ridge is slightly misleading as a description of their destination – Dixie and Tommy Thompson actually lived a few miles away, over the Connecticut border in New Canaan, then as now a stinkingly affluent suburb about an hour from Manhattan. (Paul Simon and Glenn Beck are among several of its current residents, and its tree-lined avenues served as locations for the films *The Ice Storm* and *Revolutionary Road*.) Here the Christiansens settled into a self-contained wing of the Thompsons' farm and my father took up a place at St Luke's, a posh local private school run on the English model.

Glancing through the extraordinary cache of letters he went on to send to his adored father in

England, you might think that my father had a ball over the next two years – top of the class, female admirers, the latest movies and a swanky delight in his status as a clever Brit. But I wonder if that is the whole story.

The tone of these screeds, efficiently typed on wafer-thin airmail paper, with their insouciant bravado and momentary lapses into faltering boyhood, makes me think of his contemporary Holden Caulfield, hero of JD Salinger's *The Catcher in the Rye* – someone else trying extremely hard to conceal his anxiety, both about himself and the world.

Virtually everything I know about my father has come to me mediated through the memories of others, so these American letters hold enormous fascination as the only substantial first-hand evidence I have of his voice and personality. They were given to me by a thoughtful cousin who unearthed them in some bottom drawer when Little Holland Hall was being cleared out after Brenda sold the place in her dotage, and I have read them over many times, searching in vain for clues or even clews – threads which could link me umbilically to him. But on this batsqueak frequency all I can pick up is someone trying to prove himself to a geographically distant but persistently dominant father. Look at me, Daddy, he is saying, I'm ready. I can do this, I can take adulthood in my stride. At least, I think I can.

Some of Brenda's letters to Chris have survived too, charting the family's first weeks in New Canaan and the hoo-ha of settling in. The combination of egoism and indolence they evince is ludicrous to the point of being distasteful. Given the draconian restrictions on currency export and exchange, money is a worry, so she visits the St Regis in Manhattan to meet up with Alfred Hitchcock:

> *who said that if I needed any dough I wasn't to worry at all. He could help me all I wanted. He took me aside and said How much do you want Brenda? – I'll send you a cheque for 1,000 dollars to be going on with. So far it hasn't arrived but I expect he had to wait until he got back to Hollywood.*

The cheque did eventually arrive, but she continues to find that 'dollars vanish like Indian rope tricks'. Her bank balance aside, she writes blithely that 'we are having a lovely time, like one perpetual holiday', basking in the summer heat, swimming in ponds, playing backgammon and picnicking in the woods.

Yet the next letter reports that their hostess-landlady Dixie Tighe – a creature 'famous for her blunt language and flamboyant lifestyle' who later became a war correspondent in Europe – was becoming visibly irritated with the Christiansen children. Brenda contemplates leaving them with Dixie, because 'they seem to take no notice of me whatsoever' and 'I feel that T[ommy]-D[ixie] must feel that if the mother wasn't about they could control [them] better.'

With the Blitz raining mayhem over London, this was scarcely a possibility. So instead Brenda took to wallowing in bed, playing at her hobby of 'colouring photos … a nice pastime for the winter months'. 'I go to bed mostly about 8.30 or 9', she explains, and 'I get up late as there isn't a thing else to do.'

On New Year's Eve, as a consequence of a fireside conversation with Dixie, she roused herself with a whimsical plan to open a fish and chip shop in nearby Stamford. 'I intend to visit a Scotch fish and chip in Brooklyn to have a chat with the man – if he is still there to find out how much the equipment is,' she fantasises. 'I am going to experiment with batter – and also frying chips in cotton oil – and salting them before wrapping them up. As the man used to do outside mother's flat in Acton. Then I'm going to see how much rents are in Stamford – how much potatoes cost a sack – or a cwt – and then I'll write to Hitch[cock] and see what he thinks of it – AND I shall get someone to run the business side of it for me – maybe Alice Rogers – she is wonderful and very practical. I have just rung Alice – and she says she thinks it is a most wonderful idea – and she'll do everything to help – and will do the business end of it for me – and look after the money part – and also help fry if necessary.'

At which point Brenda bids her husband an off-hand good night, with a casual farewell postscript 'about the last raid on London – I didn't know about it – until Dix rang me to say that you were O.K. Gosh, St Bride's church – and having to dynamite all around you today – Christ – where will it end – and my only consolation is that when the war started we all thought that London would go in a day.' Gosh indeed!

No more is heard about the chippie scheme, or the multi-tasking Alice Rogers. Two months later, however, Brenda reports that the children have succumbed en masse to chicken pox. She admits that she hopes to contract it herself too, because another more pressing challenge has presented itself. 'I've been roped in to represent Poundridge [sic] in the great nation wide drive for the British war relief – and I'm terrified. I am the head of the district, and am supposed to find women to work under me – or girls – and as the woman said as she talked me into it, Brenda and her change of life ladies. NO ONE in this district seems to want to help at all.' And perhaps nobody did, because this scheme seems to have evanesced too.

With a mother so deeply adrift, my father had to step forward and move fast. In contrast to her slackness and passivity – it is almost as though she cannot believe that all this is happening to her – his tone is urgent, his version of events action-packed. He is on the qui vive, he knows he has been dealt a strong hand and must make the most of the opportunities. Yes, he was unbelievably fortunate to be where he was, but in his way he was brave too. What a vast rite of passage he had to negotiate over two and a half years, from the rambling pencilled letter describing the Atlantic crossing in July 1940 to the confidently typed final letter of December 1942.

It's a rather wan little boy who writes to his father that after leaving London, he had sat with his family on the train 'very depressed so drinking champagne to keep the spirits up. It did after about 10 minutes. Then everybody except me started to write letters to you saying, we are on the boat, but we are still on the train.' Soon he is more cheerful, however, relating in exhausting detail every aspect of the liner's fiixtures and fittings as well as offering goggle-eyed accounts of lavish meals and encounters with fellow refugees in the lounge after dinner. 'One night I was approached by a Polish girl who said to me, "How old are you?" (A) "13". Then she said "I thought you were about 20." Then she said to me, "Do you dance?" I replied "No". Rather amusing episode, don't you think?'

Arriving in New York for the first time, he is blasé – 'I did not feel the slightest bit of exhilaration, in fact I was slightly bored: the great skyline had no effect.' And no sooner has he unpacked his bags than he turns his eye to the American press. 'In the *Daily News* I saw something that might be rather useful to you. Instead of putting the date at the top of the page put it down the side.'

Could he really have been so obnoxious? And before you read on, let me tell you that the comeuppance you may think he deserves doesn't come up. Six months later and still 13, he may have calmed down a bit, but the sheen of urbane sophistication has not tarnished and he hasn't even had his face slapped.

Brenda's relations with the volatile Dixie became openly fractious. In relaying various trivial domestic skirmishes to her husband, she starts referring to her landlady drily as 'Madame' and deploring the short fuse of her hot temper. The arrangement was clearly unravelling, but since Tommy Thompson was an employee of the *Daily Express*, some semblance of decorum had to be maintained. Fortunately for Brenda, Hitler decided to turn his attentions eastwards, allowing her to return to Britain in October 1941.

Quite who was left in loco parentis is never made clear from the letters. Presumably Dixie kept some sort of pseudo-maternal eye on these four orphans and perhaps a warm-hearted cookie-baking shirt-washing mammy slaved in the kitchen. But if such a personage did exist, she is never mentioned. The overwhelming impression is that it was my fourteen-year-old father who assumed primary responsibility.

I would be very obliged if you would inform the children that I am no longer an ogre. They still recoil from my grasp when I try to put in shirt tails, help them find their homework by questioning them on my knee, and occasionally offer a little advice on being good and doing homework in a proper place. Apparently my former wrongdoings have left too great an impression, and I am forced to conscript your aid. This is sure to bring on a lecture about bullying, being tolerant and remembering that they are not all as big as I am ... I suggest that you instill a little competitive spirit in them in a few letters. That brings me to letters. Your correspondence is shameful. Here we are writing you letters every weekend and we seem to hear from you about once a month. If the mail is bad, send them by boat too. All you need is a piece of carbon paper.

PS, he adds, after this tirade, 'I have a peachy subject for my next letter – my philosophy of life, which is beginning to take shape.' What this might be has not survived – if indeed it was ever hatched – but he announces in the next letter that he has 'nation-alistic tendencies, probably as a result of American idealism' and can 'proudly recall rapping some fellow on the head because he didn't stand at atten-tion during the national anthem'. A few months later he lets fall 'the suspicion I consider myself Hamlet'.

But neither an existential crisis, mother-hen clucking over his siblings nor the rumblings of war are at the forefront of his mind. Girls are the problem: oh, how they get in the way of a fellow, but what can you do? 'I have a feeling the B+ in English [a disap-pointment] had something to do with les femmes. I have received a Valentine but the romantic value is nil because I know who it came from and she is a suet pudding à la Prussian … Am now going to hear Rudy Vallee so that I can pick up some tips for the next date. Sometimes I sing to 'em.'

To a school dance he invites Jane, who 'works in New York as a shop girl in a wholesale fabric and wallpaper store. She is very pleasant and awfully easy to get along with … but about twelve o' clock all her lustre disappeared'. To the next hop he squires one Ethel, who is succeeded 'on a blind' by Gloria. However, it is Judy who seems to be his prime target. She is not easy prey: in fact, she flounces about, in two minds about him.

For four months I have been doing everything to

make her take a little more interest ... I seem doomed
to become crazy over older girls until I catch up with
myself. I don't care how much younger I may be, I
have known Judy for over a year and I am not going
to give up a wonderful girl like that without a fight. I
am now waiting with bated breath to see if she accepts
my invitation to the Christmas dance. She was going
to make it up but some nitwit repeated something I
had said all twisted and she was presumably upset.
Anything in the world will upset that girl.

In the end, his Christmas dance date was another
unnamed girl, 'on a blind' which turned out 'so so'.
Reviewing 1942 over Christmas, this 15-going-on-
25-year-old decides that Judy has been the most
important thing in it, 'because it was my first real
affair' – the past tense being key here.

The other persistent theme through 1942 is the
school magazine, the *St Luke's Sentinel*, of which
one yellowing edition survives in my possession.
His nemesis here was a guy named King Whitney,
nominally the editor, but 'the laziest devil that ever
happened' who leaves all the real work to his hungry,
competent but unfooled underling assistant editor.
My father makes a great meal of it all. Clutching
his brow and beating his breast, he deals with his
onerous responsibilities to this publication, enduring
the headaches of negotiating with recalcitrant student
journalists as well as processing their rotten copy

into something publishable (his only signed contri-
bution is a surprisingly straight-faced account of the
school's air-raid drills). He can take the pressure, but
Jeez, is it hard and he's nobody's patsy.

*I am now doing a surly revolt. I refuse to be the
jack-of-all-trades for the sheet. Any articles that
need writing, be written again, torn up, any business letters that have to be written all are given the
same approach. 'Michael, you are the backbone of
the Sentinel. If you weren't there we wouldn't have a
paper, would we, Whitney?' Whitney growls. 'Well
Michael, we want an article on the dance.' So now
instead of cheerfully saying 'Yes', I say, 'Not my
department.'*

All of this shows him rehearsing for the role he
already dreams of assuming – the editorship of a daily
paper as magnificent as his father's *Daily Express*. He
is as proud of his efforts as he is ashamed of them,
and desperate to know if his father thinks what he
has produced is any good or not. 'With my eyes shut,
I enclose the Sentinel,' he writes gingerly. 'I had no
idea a paper could be so awful. When it came out
there was nearly a revolution … If you read it from
the back the effect will be much pleasanter.'

Chris's verdict has not come down to posterity
but looking at the *Sentinel* now, I would say: it's
fine, just fine, calm down. It's the school magazine,

for heaven's sake. But my father gets increasingly hysterical. 'Sending you another Sentinel. I have no excuses, no alibis, nothing. It might have been worse, but we didn't have enough material to fill fourteen pages, but had ads for that number. That is the reason why page thirteen is composed completely of little bits written after the paper had been made up. Mr Kidd did a great deal of work on this, but even so the news coverage is awful.'

Although one might suppose that so much smart talk from a gangling six-foot alien scoring straight As in everything from English to deportment would have irritated the hell out of his contemporaries, he seems to have been much liked at St Luke's, and even in a country where the young tend to rate conformity as the cardinal virtue, he was hailed as a great character and a bold original.

Gleefully he reports that one master, a Mr Graves, describes him as 'the most self-confident nitwit in the school'. The insult is clearly affectionate, even though some of his more pretentious transatlantic witticisms ('I have always thought that the Left Book Club was a sort of lost property office for books. And that the management put new covers and sold them on') would probably have gone way over Graves's head, let alone those of other tenth-graders. But that sort of remark was the result of the top-table diet on which he had been fed: who else at St Luke's would have received from their fathers at Christmas anything so *mondaine* as a copy of the latest volume of James Agate's diaries?

For all the latent insecurity, all the showing off and trying too hard, all the *blague* and bluster (and liberal recourse to a thesaurus), there must have been something infectious about his free spirit, his gaiety and energy. In the end, I am charmed. How, for instance, can one not smile at this paragraph from a letter of December 1942, when he takes the train into Manhattan and plays at being a flâneur on the Avenues?

Two weeks ago, on Bill's Thanksgiving Holiday I spent the weekend in New York with him. We just seemed to walk and walk and walk and walk. Walked from Grand Central to the defense exhibition, walked two hours round that and then had a meal because I was literally having cramp in the stomach. Had to have two main courses, to appease my appetite. Then Bill found out the Austrian friend of his who had fixed up a bowling party had bowled already, and suggested we should go to a German movie. Never. So Bill went to a girl's place he knew, and we had dinner and sat through The Reluctant Dragon and Navy Blues. About twelve o'clock we got them home and then oh! walk of walks, I had to go from twenty-first to forty-second to get my case. Walked it, waking up half Lexington Avenue with

my rendering of Bulldog, Bulldog, wow, wow, wow,
Eli, Yale. Crawled into Bill's apartment at 1.15
and plopped asleep as though I had gone Christmas
shopping at Selfridges.

The letters home stop abruptly at the end of 1942. I don't know what happened next and despite scouring the relevant passenger lists, I have been unable to discover why, how or precisely when he and his siblings returned to Britain – via Portugal and Ireland? – on what must have been a dangerous and terrifying journey, even if it did take place after the Battle of the Atlantic was effectively over in mid-1943. I don't even know where he finished his education, if indeed he went back to school at all. The possibility of university is never mentioned, but in those days it wasn't the obvious primary option that it is now for bright young men. All I do know is that when he arrived back in Britain he would not have seen his father for nearly three years; that at the end of the war he was in Liverpool, doing his National Service in the navy; and that in 1947 he began work on the *Daily Mail*, where he met a young woman reporter, my mother Kathleen Lyon.

My mother, yes. Well, she came from a background very different from that of the Christiansens. Her milieu was one for which the adjective 'respectable' might have been coined. It would be very difficult to make it sound interesting, because in any novelistic sense it isn't. The Lyons and the Duncans (my grandmother's patronymic) came from the same area of the nation's skeleton, the unbreakable backbone of the provincial middle-middle classes – a region that no modern social analyst has ever adequately explored or dramatised. The Lyons and the Duncans are pretty much what they seem to be. Back into the 1850s, as far as I can trace them, neither line seems to have made any significant move socially upwards or downwards, all their careers, marriages and children merely endorsing the solidity of their status as a succession of small businessmen and professionals of Scots ancestry who did well but not very well.

Blamelessly upstanding and quietly couth, one up on the ladder from the Pooters, unblemished by any scandal (except one hushed-up Victorian, rumoured in Lyon lore to have killed himself with a gulp of prussic acid on hearing that his wife had left him), they offer nothing heinous, nothing grotesque or glittering – a distant relation by marriage to the Earl of Clanmorris (said to be the inspiration for John le Carré's George Smiley) is about the best that can be done.

With this ingrained reluctance to peep over the parapet, let alone advance into the field, the Lyons suffered from a lack of imagination and daring. My mother's brother – a Nottingham dentist who had dreamed of being a writer until he was browbeaten into training for something more reliable – often bemoaned his family's cautious attitude to existence, its want of me-first, must-have aggression, as a curse on our genome. By walking slowly and deferentially along the wall, the Lyons attempted to skirt disaster and by and large they succeeded: my grandfather Lyon even managed to avoid conscription for the First World War on the prosaic grounds of his flat feet.

This Grandfather Lyon worked all his adult life for a big London paperworks in some sales capacity, and his salary paid for a stolid house, staffed by a maid-servant, in a leafy road in Leigh-on-Sea. I do not want to paint a bleak or snobbish caricature of the sort to which such ordinariness is normally reduced. Life there was not spiritually empty or terminally tedious: there were plenty of books around and holidays were taken in Switzerland. The virtues of the household were legion. Beyond keeping clothes on in public, I never know quite what politicians mean when they talk of 'decency' as a fundamental national asset, but the Lyons had it in spades. They troubled nobody, they paid their bills on time and observed standard Church of England ethics. They were lightened up by a keen sense of humour which extended to self-mockery and a sense of emotional proportion which also allowed for displays of affection. All round, they were much, much nicer people – much less selfish, much less brash – than the Christiansens.

Ma was born in 1926, to a mother of 41, an age at which sexual activity among respectable folk was meant to have ceased and pregnancy was generally considered somewhat embarrassing. Was Ma a 'mistake' resulting from the absence of contraception or my grandfather's exceptional consumption of one too many? Whatever the explanation for her existence, her brother Duncan was eleven years older than her, her sister Jean five years older, and she grew up dimly feeling that she had not been entirely wanted, or at least not willed. Perhaps this explains her lifelong need to push and elbow in order to be heard and assert herself. She could not and would not be silent, she let nothing pass and she wanted the world's attention.

This is blatantly evident in a hilarious early photograph, in which she stands at the centre of the frame, like a tiny cuckoo in the nest, fixing the cameraman with an alarmingly enthusiastic toothy grin, while the much bigger and senior school-uniformed girls around her, including the diffident Jean, look distinctly more sheepish. Ma always had guts, she was ready to give it a go; you had to give her that. But she liked to be up at the front.

With the prospect of air raids along the Essex coast and my grandfather's typically Lyonish prognostication that Hitler was likely to win, the family moved to Aylesbury in 1940, where Ma attended the local grammar school. Like her siblings, she was very bright, with a special passion for history, but her education was curtailed by the war and in 1942, at the age of sixteen, she got her first job on a local newspaper and began a giddyingly swift ascent.

Although she longed to be an actress – and might well have been a good one – a thespian bent wasn't something that the Lyons were ever going to countenance, so that dream faded. But she had read in her comic of the exploits of Pat the Girl Reporter, who rode a bicycle and solved mysteries, and like so many girls of that generation, she remained smitten by the glamour of the cinema. So it was in the sixpenny stalls on a Saturday afternoon that she was infected by the romance of journalism as a career for women and a way out and up into the world.

Women reporters were a staple of American movies in the 1930s: sharp-tongued, cynical broads like Dixie Thompson who could beat men at their own game and didn't take no for an answer. Big stars such as Joan Crawford in *Dance, Fools, Dance*, Jean Arthur in *Mr Deeds Goes to Town*, Rosalind Russell in *His Girl Friday*, Katharine Hepburn in *Woman of the Year* all gave some life to the stereotype, though it was perhaps most purely embodied in Torchy Blaine, played by Glenda Farrell, the motor-mouthed heroine of a long-running series of schlocky Warner Brothers B pictures.

Feminist cultural historians have examined the phenomenon in some detail. Magazines at that time held little allure for the likes of my mother; they were for prim and timid ladies who sat behind a baize door surrounded by other prim and timid ladies. To work on a newspaper gave you a licence to roam and stay out late, free from obvious family ties, husbands or children. A woman in this position didn't need to exploit her sexuality like a blonde femme fatale in order to get what she wanted. I suppose to a teenage girl in search of a role model 'journalist' must have had an appeal comparable to that which Helen Mirren's *Prime Suspect* character DCI Jane Tennison exerted during the 1990s.

Of course, these exciting fictions bore very little relation to the realities of the profession. Women reporters had been employed by newspapers since the late nineteenth century (Henrietta Stackpole, a character faintly patronised by Henry James in *The Portrait of a Lady*, is one of the kind) and with the rise of the yellowish tabloid press, the massifying of circulation and the burning issue of female suffrage, their bylines became more prevalent. If more women were buying and reading newspapers, it was logical that they should write them too. But only so much, so far: editors kept their lady correspondents carefully confined, rarely inviting them into the office and shutting them out from the big stories and the front pages. Domestic matters, shopping, fashion, entertainment, gossip – the lighter aspects of life – were their domain. A woman's view was always oblique: it was only men who occupied the central positions and commanded the broader perspectives.

By the 1930s, in both Britain and the US, a handful of exceptional women had been allowed out of the parlour of journalistic gentility and admitted into open news territory. They adopted two specific guises: either 'sob sisters' presenting the sentimental, emotional aspects of court cases, scandals and disasters; or 'stunt girls' entering the lion's cage or the opium den, as it were, and returning to tell the tale 'from the woman's angle'. (The great female foreign correspondents such as Martha Gellhorn transcend this latter category.)

One outstanding representative of the breed, both a sob sister and a stunt girl, was employed – and highly valued – by my grandfather Chris on the *Daily Express*. A butcher's daughter from Hull, Hilde Marchant wrote memorably vivid 'human interest' stories of the Abdication, the Spanish Civil War, the Russian invasion of Finland and the bombing of Coventry. Described by a colleague Bernard Hall as 'a tiny little thing, with wispy hair, never in place, but two major physical assets, a deep-toned, exciting voice and dark, beautiful eyes which always seemed to me to conceal a wistful wonder about the world and its mystery', she projected her own combination of frailty and resilience into the people she wrote about – victims of war and its deprivations, battling on regardless against the odds. But Hilde Marchant was a one-off: her love life was a mess, drink soon got the better of her and she would die destitute underneath the arches.

Ma had a lot of Hilde's pluck, and that quality inborn in any good reporter – brazen temerity. She was smart, beautiful, energetic, obliging, resourceful and on the ball too, but it was that readiness to barge in anywhere and ask anyone anything that must have clinched it. Nobody else in her family had that gumption, which often landed her in trouble and occasionally got her out of it; by nature, the Lyons followed everyone at a respectful distance and made as few demands of life as they could.

Brazen temerity was certainly the springboard which launched her out of the doldrums of Aylesbury. By the time she was seventeen, in 1943, she landed a cub reporter's job on a much-admired new regional evening paper, the *Oxford Mail*. Wartime conscription had cleared the field of male competitors somewhat, but achieving such a position was still quite something for anyone of her sex and age. With lodgings on the Banbury Road, she had her first taste of freedom, and she loved it. Male undergraduates of the time went wild for her – after she died I received a letter from one such, recalling her as the Zuleika Dobson of her day. She also caused a great to-do when she arrived late to report on a debate at the Oxford Union. Rather than climbing the stairs to the ladies' enclave in the gallery, she mistakenly slipped in through a door which took her straight on to the floor. No woman had ever trod those boards before – they had been a sacred male preserve since the dawn of time, and the debate had to be stopped while officers considered how to deal with this shocking interloper. She told me that eventually they had allowed her to stay, and she felt she had struck a blow for the equality of women. Sadly, however, I have been unable to find any minutes in the Union's records to corroborate her version of this earth-shattering incident.

In the autumn of 1944, when she was eighteen, brazen temerity propelled her as far as the heights of Fleet Street. As a reporter on the *Daily Mail*, she was the youngest journalist on the paper and the only woman in the newsroom. I wish I knew how she had got the job: the cuttings she kept from the *Oxford Mail* suggest diligence and confidence, but she must have radiated something more promising

My mother at eighteen

than competence in the interview. Her reward was to be flung into the thick of it.

These were heady times, as the war moved inexorably to its climax and we seemed to be winning it. Paris and Brussels had been liberated and the allies were steadily advancing east, but there was failure at Arnhem and V2s were exploding all over London.

Every morning before she clocked in at the paper, her father made her meet him at Marylebone Station, where he alighted on his way to work in the City. You might have thought a telephone call would have done the trick, but the random murderousness of the V2s must have intensified the desire for the reassurance of your own eyes – and supposing there was an hour-long queue for the only unbombed box?

Against this epic backdrop, Ma was out covering new prefabs in Hackney, queues for (and shortages of) everything from shoes to fish to soap, Yanks in London mourning Roosevelt, preparations for the return of evacuees, Britain's first female stipendiary magistrate in session, and a visit from Bob Hope. Meanwhile, her elder sister Jean was commuting from home as a nine-to-five shorthand-typist in the Ministry of Agriculture and Fisheries.

The *Daily Mail* trailed Chris's *Daily Express* in terms of both circulation and reputation, but along with the more liberal *News Chronicle*, it constituted a cornerstone of an enormous middle market for newspapers, with a reach and influence vastly wider than that of magazines (except perhaps *Picture Post*), or the BBC.

The atmosphere in their offices, concentrated around the rookery of Fleet Street, was fast-living and viciously competitive – a man's world of rough and tumble, fugged with cigarette smoke and fuelled by booze, to which women were only admitted on sufferance.

The day worked on a two-shift rhythm, with the top brass straddling both. First came the stone-cold sober morning conference and some initial planning. Reporters were then despatched to hunt the stories down, after which anyone remaining in the office went out for a long and largely liquid lunch, returning nakedly drunk but remarkably functional. In the afternoon, as copy came in, a second shift nursed typewritten sheets into layout and print, a process which would finish well after midnight, lubricated by further lashings of the hard stuff.

At least that is the prevalent myth. Sometimes I think that all this boozing is inflated to Homeric proportions in the memory of steel-livered survivors and that it's basically part of a nostalgic yarn about the good old, bad old days. But my guess is that after 2pm, one could assume an overall level of intoxication in any newspaper office that would now be considered scandalous – 'We girls drank to keep up with the lads. Gin mostly,' Drusilla Beyfus, a rookie on the *Express*'s women's page at the time, told me. 'Drinking, like everything else, was very competitive.' Writing fluently while sozzled, passing out in the loo, late-night riotousness – all this was the norm, a badge not even of honour but simply of guild membership, upgraded when one was introduced to

the watering-hole of El Vino's, a wine cellar operating virtually as a club in which unaccompanied
juniors were not welcome.

Without any women in senior or managerial positions, a teenage girl like my mother was unprotected
in this snake-pit. As one prominent female survivor
of this era told me, 'Women were considered fair
game and you had to be robust about it. When a man
pinched my bottom, I just snapped: "If you ever do
that again, I will kill you." You couldn't act the mili-
tant feminist, it just wasn't a possibility. I remember
one idiot lurching drunk into the features room,
where most of the women on the paper were congre-
gated, and shouting: "Great smell of cunt in here."
But actually that was as nasty as it got.'

Yet perhaps it could get nastier in the newsroom
among raucous reporters, where as the sole representative of her sex, my eighteen-year-old mother was
despised, resented and lusted after. Brazen temerity
came to her rescue again, and she got on with the
job regardless, secretly rather thrilled by the boys'
crass attentions. 'The only decent ones were the
pansies,' she once told me. 'They would compliment
you on a new hat or remember to ask if your cold was
better.' Peter Wildeblood, later to suffer humiliation
and imprisonment in the notorious Beaulieu 'vice'
case, was one such that she remembered fondly. But
that sort of niceness wasn't what she really wanted,

and she never had a gay best friend. Effeteness was something for which she felt disdain bordering on contempt: I don't think she ever departed from her generation's conventional view of a homosexual as something genetically less complete than a red-blooded, fully fledged male. 'How sad,' she would say with a rather irritating simper on learning that some handsome fellow liked to dance at the other end of the ballroom. 'What a waste.' She thought she was being compassionate.

Ma lived in a respectable ladies' hostel in Bayswater, of exactly the sort so acutely and comically described in all its hopeless dun-coloured dinginess by Muriel Spark in *The Girls of Slender Means*. For one guinea a week, evening meal included, she shared an attic, curtained into two cubicles, with a nice quiet receptionist called Rosalie who snored but didn't fuss. The one great drama was a girl with insoluble boyfriend problems who was discovered by Ma with her head in the communal gas oven and who had to be dragged whimpering back to life. But the other girls upstairs were a jolly lot, chortling at the silly men in their wake and unfazed by the minor vicissitudes of war.

Downstairs, where older, settled residents occupied their own rooms, lurked more formidable parties requiring delicate negotiation. Ma may have found the pansies at the *Mail* comfortable, but the

lesbian elements hereabouts – mostly large-bosomed
and clothed in some sort of military uniform, as per
the cliché – seemed predatory as they padded along
the linoleum to the freezing-cold bathroom in frayed
silk dressing gowns and mule slippers clutching their
washbags. One Wren took to banging in peremp-
tory fashion on Ma's door asking to borrow things,
another stroked her hair and called her Katey the
puss-cat, another took excessive interest in her
lingerie. Her Lyon upbringing had not prepared her
for this sort of thing.

So the war ended. As the adrenalin rush of the road to
victory faded, there was a lot of clearing-up to do and
grumbling came back into fashion. Ma chronicled it
all, acting as both sob sister and stunt girl: rationing
and coupons, heart-warming stories of family re-
unions and GI brides, the hottest April for 90 years,
the fury of the British Housewives' League, a dentist
who claimed that hypnosis could make dentistry
painless. Brazen temerity failed her only when she
got off the bus on her way back to the hostel in the
evenings and had to run the gauntlet of tarts loitering
against the railings along the Bayswater Road.

Her talents were widely noticed. The dauntingly
sophisticated and clever Lady Rothermere – then
wife to the *Mail*'s proprietor but later married to

Ian Fleming – took a shine to her and invited her to elegant dinner parties of a sort she had never before encountered, graced with cocktails, finger bowls and an etiquette for the use of cutlery. One of Ann Fleming's surviving letters (published in book form in 1985) suggests that she may have had an ulterior motive for cultivating this stripling: my mother was also subtly pumped for inside information on the mood in the newsroom.

Whether through her own merits or because Lady Rothermere whispered in an influential ear, her progress was swift. In 1947, the editor assigned her to cover the first big good-news story to emerge out of the post-war glump – Princess Elizabeth's wedding to Lieutenant Philip Mountbatten. Through the months of preparation, she shows a sharp eye for interesting detail – 'German POWs were among the most enthusiastic of the people that thronged the streets for the royal party's triumphant tour through the Border country yesterday,' for example – and treads confidently through the palaver about the dress and the reception.

I wonder if she ever considered that she was about to marry into royalty herself – albeit only the scion of a shaky, shady, upstart Fleet Street dynasty. Yet there was no doubt that in these post-war years Chris was king of the game, and my father Michael was his heir apparent, buoyed by privilege and wealth and expectations, even though he scrupulously insisted on making his way on his own merits. My mother, on the other hand, had come up from nowhere much with little baggage, and her family had shown nothing but scepticism towards her aspirations: they weren't proud of her success so much as bewildered and even frightened by it.

They met early in 1947 at the *Daily Mail*. My father had finished with the navy, passed through some sort of internship or apprenticeship on the *Liverpool Echo* and arrived in Fleet Street as a sub-editor, building on skills he had learnt with the school magazine but still a backroom boy, lower in the pecking order than my fast-ascending and slightly older mother. I don't know much about their courtship, but it was clearly a fine romance. They dined on oysters at Wheeler's in Soho and at Les Ambassadeurs in Mayfair; they saw *Oklahoma!* twice at Drury Lane – its smoochy waltz, 'People will say we're in love', became their anthem. They used up their paltry foreign currency allowance on a weekend in Paris via the Golden Arrow from Victoria, and spent a rowdy Christmas at Palais Christiansen, Holland Hall. Chris liked my mother; Brenda did not.

What role did sex play at this stage? All things were possible among young people in London whom the war had pushed as close to death as they were to life, and Larkin was only kidding about it all

Ma in her early twenties

beginning in 1963. But later in her life, my mother intimated that she regarded a shared bed as a ritual to be negotiated rather than a party to be enjoyed, and the liberations of the sixties brought out the Scots puritan in her. 'Decadence!' she tutted when we sat watching the Rolling Stones on *Ready, Steady, Go* circa 1965, as she did again when I dragged her to *Fellini Satyricon* five years later. Her romantic ideal of manhood remained a sharp-witted Battle of Britain pilot – someone brave and competent, who would nobly take the lead and fling a girl manfully on to the chaise longue – so it surprises me now that she should have fallen for anyone as generally off-the-wall as my father. I remember we had a book at home called *I Married Adventure* (it had a jazzily stylish zebra-striped cloth cover, reflective of its contents, the memoirs of a lady big-game hunter called Osa Johnson) and I guess that in that title lies the key to her choice. She was young and hot-blooded and she had to shake off the defensive slow-burn principles which kept all the other members of her family plodding on a treadmill permanently paced for the middle-aged. My father was moving fast in contrast, and that must have been exhilarating. He was not safe, and in terms of ambition, the sky wasn't even halfway to his limit.

Her other admirers – and they were legion and often abject – seem as she pictured them to have been rather more conventionally decent types, all kept at a distance from her bed. My father's precocious interest in Judy and all those other New Canaan Lolitas, on the other hand, suggests that he had a powerful libido, that he felt uninhibited in female company and that he relished the chase of skirt. Ma told me that while he had been in Liverpool doing National Service he had fallen under the spell of an older woman and that the affair had been obscurely troubling for him. Perhaps she took his virginity. Whether he took my mother's I have no idea.

Editing the *Daily Express* left Chris with little time for hobbies, but he enjoyed the top-grade luxury toy of a home movie camera, and he particularly enjoyed recording his family en fête. Among several of his surviving reels is a brief colour film of my parents' wedding at St Mary Abbots, Kensington, in September 1948.

We imagine those post-war years to have passed in a sludge, and the formal black-and-white pictures in the wedding album evoke to me only a grey, slow world of utility and rations. Yet the flickering images captured by Chris's camera are vibrant with colour: the familiar tomato red of a passing bus, the purple of my grandmother's suit, the sky blue of the bridesmaids' dresses, the sky blue of the sky, come to that.

And there is my father, already balding at 21, lanky in morning dress and Mr Magoo specs, blinking at the sunshine as he emerges grinning from the Christiansen townhouse in Barton Street. Cut to the corner of Kensington High Street and a gaggle of shoppers stopping outside the church opposite Barker's to watch the bride's arrival. Cut to the bridesmaids: my two paternal aunts and my mother's elder sister Jean, herself then still unmarried and looking faintly peeved and green-eyed at having to walk up the aisle behind a younger sibling who appeared to have hit the marital jackpot. Cut to a parade of relations looking fifteen years younger than I remember them, and some of whom I do not recognise at all. Cut to my mother, stepping out of a limousine, holding a cascade of red roses, looking magically beautiful, poised yet nervous, and reluctant to be the centre of attention. She is on the arm of her handsome father, who for a moment stares quizzically into Chris's lens as if asking the question: to what am I giving my daughter away?

Christiansens on the left; Lyons on the right

2.

The newly weds lived at first in a tiny dank flat at the top of one of the few houses in Holland Park that hadn't been devastated by the Luftwaffe. Theirs was a shabby world of fitful gas rings and tins of powdered milk, overcast with the pall of Stafford Cripps' screw-tight housekeeping. One of the first domestic ordeals my mother had to weather was entertaining the in-laws for dinner. Her culinary skills were at that time absolutely minimal, but for this occasion, table linen and cut glass had to be acquired and – ration books be damned – fancy stops pulled out in order to keep Brenda happy: her standards were sophisticated, her tastes whimsical, and she wasn't someone with the imagination to make sympathetic allowances or award an encouraging A for effort. Gin-heavy cocktails were served and something Frenchified in a white sauce thickened with condensed milk was the *plat*, painstakingly drawn from the *Good Housekeeping* kitchen bible.

My father insisted on regarding the whole exercise as high drawing-room comedy, but Ma was petrified – Brenda's rapier-sharp tongue had an exquisite capacity to lash out a thoughtlessly wounding remark. The menu passed muster, but only just: nothing nasty was said, but nothing nice either.

Every morning after breakfast, before he left for work, my mother would hear my father nervously vomiting in the lavatory. Anxiety was something he was otherwise crafty at hiding, but behind all his cocked-hat debonair insouciance and daft irresponsibility, he was so driven and desperate to get to the top that every day he felt he had to be on his guard, armed to fight his patch and make his mark.

My mother had a weak chest and although she survived the rigours of the winter of 1947, she was weakened by a bad bout of jaundice and succumbed to the still endemic disease of tuberculosis a year later. She would never talk in any detail about the ensuing ordeal – it remained one of those areas of the past to which she felt unreconciled – and having read a lot about the treatments in use at the time, I can understand the shudder that seemed to electrify her whenever conversation came close to mentioning it.

What I can piece together is this. She was assigned to a private sanatorium somewhere outside Bournemouth. Throughout quiet wooded areas of suburban England lurked hundreds of these institutions – well-intentioned prisons encased in stony Edwardian mansions, discreetly screened by dense avenues of rhododendrons and shaded by louring pines. None of the locals wanted them there; the proximity of a sanatorium depressed property prices since there was real fear of contagion. Patients were accommodated under a matron and starchy nurses (several of them tubercular themselves) in small wards, some in the house, some in annexed chalets, bleakly furnished with white cast-iron bedsteads covered with coarse bedlinen and stand-ard-issue blankets. The smell of Dettol was ubiqui-tous, permeating the air.

The tedium must have been as excruciating as any physical pain. All superfluous noise was suppressed, and a mood of deadened tranquillity enforced. Even ordinary conversation was discouraged: any stim-ulus or agitation, it was thought, could inflame deli-cate lungs and damage them further. A fortunate few whose condition was not so grave were allowed an hour sitting out on the veranda or even a slow turn around the grounds. Others were given the distrac-tion of repetitive handicraft work – raffia, knitting, petit point, none of which my virtually dyspraxic mother, who struggled even to thread a needle, could get her fingers round.

The daily inertia was only punctuated by the endless succession of large-portioned meals served off squeaking trolleys on thick white plates: a full-fat breakfast, coffee and cake, three-course dinner, sugared tea and biscuits, two-course supper, a hot milky drink – everything boiled and pulped and mashed, bulked up with stodge and coated in grease. The eating cure, which didn't work.

And day and night, as if to scorn the regime of silence, came the volleys of coughing, breaking out, crackling like gunfire – rasping and raucous and rattling or hard and sharp – with the sputum evacuated into enamelled tin bowls.

My mother's case was considered bad: there was talk of putting her into an iron lung. Then, miraculously, from America, like an angel, came streptomycin, the first antibiotic decisively to destroy the infection. At first a conservative medical establishment put up some resistance, but the news of its rapidly healing effect on younger cases was very encouraging, and the ability of the editor of the *Daily Express* to make a few phone calls to high places and Harley Street ensured that his daughter-in-law was among the first to receive the drug, saving her from a terrible living death, or worse.

After the sanatorium, sickbed and maternity hospital, my mother required a gentle and stress-free convalescent environment. My father had put a deposit down on a rather grand early-Victorian terraced house in Gloucester Crescent in Camden

Town, subsequently acquired and occupied for many years by Alan Bennett. I can never pass it now without a pang of regret, and wonder wistfully how it might all have panned out for me if I'd been a child of NW1 in its fashionable heyday, with smart-talking pot-puffing intellectuals like Jonathan Miller or Jill Tweedie as next-door neighbours. But the street wasn't in its heyday then – far from it, in fact – and before either the property boom or the vogue for creative renovation, buying up anywhere so rambling, decrepit, mildewed and porous was seen not as canny investment but as an inexplicable folly which would cause you nothing but trouble and expense. Far better to plump for something waterproofed and twentieth century with reliable amenities, even if that meant submitting to the dreary routine of commuting.

So my parents opted for the 'leafy' and untroubled South London suburb of Petts Wood, where they bought an unprepossessing three-bedroomed semi-detached house in 1954. Its late trains from Charing Cross and London Bridge suited my father's crazy working hours in Fleet Street, and the fresh Kentish air and decent municipal facilities suited my mother's delicate chest and the rearing of a baby born that year and named (to my eternal mortification) in homage to the *Daily Express*'s hugely popular cartoon strip, tracking the adventures of an anthropomorphic bear in a livery of checked trousers and jumper. In other respects, however, Petts Wood would prove a disastrously inappropriate choice, offering a way of life that neither my mother nor father wanted or understood, and both of them would eventually kick violently against it.

I feel shy of adding to all the material – John Updike's novels, Mike Leigh's movies, soap operas galore – devoted over the last half-century to unpicking the pathology of suburbia or playing the all too easy game of knocking its values and exposing its hypocrisies. But the sort of safety and comfort it offered isn't everything: there's something small about the name of Petts Wood, isn't there? Something which tells you not to get your hopes up, something drastically circumscribed.

To call it a place set in aspic would just be another cliché, but it would be true to say that through the twenty years of my early life during which I was based there absolutely nothing of significance changed. This meticulously faked village, perched between the slightly more open-ended towns of Bromley and Orpington on the edge of the Kentish North Downs, serenely masqueraded as a pastoral idyll, giving a deep and necessary illusion of security to people who had grown up through the war in conditions of radical insecurity – that, I believe, was the secret of its undoubted success.

But Petts Wood does have a modest history. Until the twentieth century, it was an ancient forest, exploited as a source of timber for the Thames estuary shipyards of Woolwich and Deptford. William Willett, a successful property developer who had bought Camden Place (the house previously occupied and made famous by the exiled Emperor Napoleon III and his ghastly wife Eugénie) in nearby Chislehurst, liked to ride there at dawn and it was here, so he claimed, that he stumbled on the idea of Daylight Saving: a pamphlet that he subsequently published on the subject led directly to parliamentary debate and the institution of British Summer Time in 1916. Most of this pleasant woodland remains, handed to the National Trust in honour of Willett's memory, but in the early 1930s some of its fringes and surrounding farmland were sold for residential development, constructed along the idealistic model of Letchworth, Port Sunlight and other experimental communities of the garden suburb movement. A new railway station and shopping centre were part of the package of what the estate agents' prospectuses described as a 'sylvan town with birds, trees, flowers … *rus in urbe* … most satisfying to those of artistic taste'.

A set of unifying aesthetic criteria was estab-lished – low building density, no bungalows, every-thing to be built of brick, stone or rough-cast with pitched roofs. Many roads were lined entirely with pretentious but desirable 'cottages' in the fashionable pseudo-Tudor style, marked by dark wooden beams set into white walls, lozenged leaded windows, oak front doors and inglenook fireplaces – all symbols evoking ancient entitlement, which fed the cravings of an aspiring middle class. One of the most baronially grandiose of these fantasies (complete, it was said, with a dungeon which doubled up as a wine cellar) had been rented by General de Gaulle during the first stage of his wartime exile. Swiss-chalet-style semis and white-walled modernist flatroofers also featured, slightly lower down the price and social ladder.

Unlike Letchworth or Port Sunlight, Petts Wood hadn't benefited from a single overall master-plan, but either through the enlightened self-restraint of the developers or the nous of the local authorities, it managed to grow easily without the template of grids, straight lines and serried rows which can make London suburbs so relentless. Its better streets curved elegantly along gentle contours: everything and everybody had room to breathe. Trees, hedges and greenswards flourished alongside the herbaceous borders – gardens were of generous scale, both at the front and the rear, and their maintenance to a high standard of manicured neatness was as socially compulsory as keeping the peace. Nature, one felt, had not been pushed out, only politely invited to engage in partnership.

Shops were still genteel and individually owned, with names like Bon Ton, Gladys' Pantry and Coiffure by Arnold, late of Bond Street. The only chain stores I recall were David Greig, a precursor of Sainsbury's which functioned as a counter grocery, and a branch of Woolworth's, patronising which was considered infra dig. Should one require new clothing, a bus ride to Bromley dropped you at a branch of Marks and Spencer, but domestic morality was focused on mending rather than acquiring. I don't think that the sixties – that glibly packaged but leaky concept – meant anything much here beyond racier pop music, tighter trousers and shorter skirts; perhaps a change of heart and mind finally took hold in the seventies, by which time we had moved on.

Meanwhile everything ran on subliminal time-tables which there was nothing to impede. You could have set your watch by the daily arrival of the postman and milkman or the paper boy. Shops opened strictly from nine to five, with early closing on Wednesday. Graffiti was a word unheard of, and nobody dropped litter. The National Health Service seemed to function seamlessly too: if you felt ill, you went along to your doctor's surgery in the morning and waited half an hour or so until he saw you. He was usually smoking and invariably affable, and he knew all about you without consulting a computer screen. His subsequent workload seemed viable too: anyone confined to bed would be visited later that same day, even if it was just a matter of German measles or flu. Hospitals were run by matrons rather than managers and were squeaky clean and efficient, albeit somewhat bleak and unsophisticated. When – and why – did it all become as preposterously expensive and complex as rocket science?

Fear in this environment was something distant: I was surprised to discover a couple of years ago that because of its proximity to Biggin Hill airfield, hub of the Battle of Britain, and an important railway junction, Petts Wood had been heavily bombed by the Luftwaffe. By the time I was sentient, not a stray brick or hole remained, and nobody ever mentioned to me the 110 explosions of 1940, 1941 and 1944, one of them almost exactly opposite our house and one of which killed 35 people.

Instead I grew up with less imminent anxieties – Communist spies, the barely thawing Kremlin and a nuclear apocalypse – which for the most part could be mentally shelved. Closer to home, crime was an irritant rather than a worry: the local paper reported few splits in the social fabric deeper than shoplifting, broken windows or stolen bicycles, although the occasional flurry of indecent behaviour in a public lavatory may have caused some poor devils to stare into a hopeless abyss. Europeans were, on a sliding scale, all suspicious quantities – the Germans a defeated enemy, the French slippery, the Italians and Spanish slimy – but all we needed to do was look down on them a bit, still confident in the imperial assumption that we had won the war and the British were Best, even if the Yankees (honorary Brits) held the purse strings and called the shots.

So there we were, and it is not meet to complain. Compared with 99.9999 per cent of the entire human race since the dawn of time, Petts Woodies, fostered by the post-war Welfare State dispensation, were basking in clover and rolling in catnip. We were so free from care we could have been God's chosen race. Even though all else in creation might crumble or melt, Petts Wood, in its little way, would endure any knocks and deliver on its promises.

But there were in fact two Petts Woods: 'our' Petts Wood, which thought of itself as perpetually established and impregnably entitled, and the other Petts Wood, only a decade or so younger but more densely and cheaply built. Being separated from 'us' by the railway line, it was literally and metaphorically the other side of the tracks, referred to by 'us' as 'the tuppenny side', and considered a region where people were 'common' and the source and cause of whatever minor frictions and infractions emerged.

In his excellent *History of Petts Wood*, Peter

Waymark reports a wonderfully bracing and Blimpish speech made by the splendidly monik-ered Conservative MP Sir Waldron Smithers at the opening of the village's Embassy Cinema on the tuppenny side in 1936. It still seems to me to sum up so much about the place that I would get to know a quarter of a century later.

> *I hear there are two parts of Petts Wood. There are the people who live on this side of the railway line and the people who live on the other and I am told they don't get on well. What utter nonsense that all is! You are all Britishers, you all stood up just now for the National Anthem ... and you all have me for your Member of Parliament, whether you like it or not ... Just as if it matters which side of the dear old Southern railway you live!*
>
> *I suggest that you do something about it. People who live in number 23 in a road this side should invite a family from some number 23 on the other side to tea on a Sunday afternoon ...*

A fond dream, an idle socialistic whim! Petts Wood was too far gone for that sort of healing balm, being profoundly and incurably infested by an invis-ible skein of class markers, proliferating like malig-nant cells. The road you lived in, the food you ate, the clothes you wore, whether you pursed your lips for prunes and prism, whether you went to the toilet or nipped to the loo: all these signified, as they did throughout the country at a time when the game of U and non-U, popularised by Nancy Mitford, was a major cultural phenomenon, both an anxiety and a joke.

To imagine a system enclosing this would, I think, be misleading, inasmuch as there wasn't a grid that you could navigate or a ladder you could scale. Class didn't bludgeon or brand you: there wasn't a badge on your breast, or a flash on your shoulder. It was just something in the air, like an ectoplasm or virus – something you could never quite put your finger on and certainly not something that could be precisely engineered or controlled or quantified (Marxist analysis got this wrong). 'Breeding' was an important word hereabouts too, now altogether archaic and even then spoken in slightly hushed, masonic tones – used not in a strictly reproductive sense but in relation to etiquette, comportment and dialect as well as ultimate moral calibre. Good breeding, the mark of our Petts Wood – or so it liked to think – was a debased version of what Chaucer's knight would have called gentilesse and the Victorians gentleman-liness. There were some things that a person with this x factor would just never do (and that included mentioning the toilet). People on the tuppenny side had no breeding.

The other disease of Petts Wood, related to class

but perhaps even more debilitating, was its obsession with front. The cliché is that the suburbs have always been about 'keeping up with the Joneses', but that makes its inhabitants sound far more greedy, competitive and aspirational than they were. The point vis-à-vis the Joneses was far more a matter of maintaining one's defences, of not letting go or letting on. You didn't want them to know you were in need or pain or trouble. Everything had to seem just fine: on the tuppenny side, people had net curtains that not only twitched but also implied one might have something to hide. In our Petts Wood, houses seemed to offer themselves up for inspection, with the windows left transparent, as if to symbolise the pure state of our souls and the blamelessness of our conduct.

Front was also emotional. Once over the age of eight, there were to be no tears in public – among the truly manly, the stiff upper lip didn't even tremble. To lie might be better than to confess, if you could get away with it; no questions would be asked; nobody wanted to examine or even think about your dirty laundry. To be a nosey parker was virtually a criminal offence. The mantra was 'mind your own business': a principle for which there is, of course, much that is positive to be said. But its flip side was a refusal to get involved and a denial of any responsibility for one's neighbours – beyond the loan of a pint of milk or a lift to the station. We lived amicably side by side, but not together. That was the limit of the social contract. You could glibly but not inaccurately sum it up by asserting that Petts Wood managed the magic trick of demanding conformity while refusing community.

Into this strangely nowhere nothing place, suspended halfway between city and country, with its faked past and shallow present, came my mother and father and me, their baby son. The evidence my sister and I have for this latter part of their marriage is exiguous. How much can one read into the story that he smuggled a copy of Henry Miller's criminally pornographic *Tropic of Cancer* back from the US, but confiscated it from my mother when she started reading it? He was jealous of her motherhood: she told me that once that he had challenged her with 'I think you love that child more than you love me,' and perhaps she did as she was biologically directed. He was terrible with money too, gambling compulsively on the horses and letting it slip through his fingers like sand. In 1956, he had moved from the *Daily Mail* to the *Daily Mirror*, where he became assistant editor and worked crazily long hours, often returning home long after midnight and leaving my mother lonely and unsupported. I look back now through the prism of what I know and marvel at the unthinking way in which his life was being pushed forward while hers was being pulled back: a dynamic that obtained throughout society and which lies at the heart of everything that Betty Friedan dissected in *The Feminine Mystique*.

But for all that, the only document that survives from these years of their marriage suggests great love.

The *Mirror* appears to have sent my father on a mission to the US with the aim of investigating American schools of journalism, and in December 1957, he wrote to her. From the Gotham Hotel in New York, his teenage stomping ground, he began:

> *My darling own bear, I've just walked down Broadway at 6.30 in the evening thinking of you all the way. Perhaps you woke up at 1.30 in the morning last night and got my message – I love you and miss you very much. Yes, darling, that's absolutely true. There's nobody to tell my adventures to except you.*

He signs off: 'You are the most wonderful wife anybody could wish for.'

From the Conrad Hilton Hotel in Chicago a week later he calls her 'My beautiful darling' and writes that:

> *Time is beginning to rush by now and soon we will be together again. How wonderful if you could be with me and I could hold your hand and tell you how*

much I love you and look at that lovely little boy of ours. Always yours, Michael.

In the next letter, the ache has become more urgent and his emotion pantingly insecure:

You probably don't believe me, but it's true when I say that I am constantly thinking of you & trying to will you to know that I love you & that you mean everything to me, I wish I could know that you are well & that everything's all right. I love you, I love you, darling. Don't forget me.

A friend of mine offered a contrarian reading of these outpourings, arguing that they suggest that he had left her in doubt and that he is trying to reassure her, but this isn't an interpretation I accept: I have to believe that his ardour is sincere, because I need to think that they did know happiness together, which is what made what followed so doubly painful.

In brief: shortly after his return from this American trip, my mother became pregnant with my sister, who was born in November 1958. Eight months later, he came home and told her that he had fallen in love with his secretary Christina Robinson and that he was leaving Petts Wood to live with her. Such is love, that capricious blind Cupid and his wanton darts.

He left nothing behind except some books (*Tropic*

Christmas at Holland Hall, 1949?, my parents on
the left, Chris at the head of the table holding an
unidentified baby

of Cancer not among them), a few photographs
(mainly recording his participation in Sunday afternoon cricket matches) and one inexplicable pair of
navy-blue, white-dotted socks.

For some months afterwards, he would come back
to Petts Wood from wherever it was he was living
on his free afternoons and take me out. Of where
we went, what we did or what was said, I have no

recollection. One day, however, he left me waiting outside my nursery school for an hour. Everyone else had gone home, and he hadn't telephoned to warn anyone. I was terribly upset (and it is true that throughout my life I have been absurdly, sometimes hysterically anxious when anyone in my life fails to turn up at the appointed hour) and at the handover moment, my mother did not spare him the vitriol.

'If you can't come on time, I said, then don't come at all. So he scuttled off like a frightened rabbit and never came back. Never.' This is the story she told, and certainly I never saw or communicated with him again. But I have only her word for it, and there must be more to it than that.

———————

Anger and shame became the two driving motors of my mother's life after my father left her. Anger is the easy bit to understand and imagine – she nobly kept it from my sister and me, but to friends and confidantes she was often a wailing banshee of resentment, grief and paranoia, tossed and tormented by the peculiarly intense and sulphurous hatred spawned by love betrayed. Revenge came in the shape of divorce court justice. She appointed a top City solicitor, Rex Paynter of Devonshire and Co, who clearly fought her corner brilliantly and who went back to the courts at least twice over the years as my father

fecklessly neglected to pay up according to the stipu-
lations of the settlement. His favourite trick with the
school fees, my mother would sneer, was to buy time
by sending a cheque to the bursar but rendering it
unbankable by misdating it. I never knew this until
much later, but at one point my prep school had to
wait for over four terms for its bill to be settled – that
it did so without complaining or threatening to turf
me out is eternally to its credit.

My father's family became the victim of a lot
of my mother's displaced hostility and paranoia.
I am sure they tried in their rough and ready way
to be kind and sympathetic, expressing shock and
dismay at what Michael had done, and I certainly
never heard any of them express any great warmth
towards Christina Robinson. Even the bottomlessly
shallow Brenda roused herself – like the supine Lady
Bertram in *Mansfield Park*, whom she greatly resem-
bled in several respects, she was not so deep-dyed in
her egotism to 'think little of guilt and infamy' and
she admitted to my mother that her son had behaved
'without honour'.

But after all he was theirs, and their loyalties
had to remain with him. Whatever they said to my
mother was going to end up being the wrong thing
and however hard they tried, she was not going to let
them lay claim to me, their first-born grandson, or
my baby sister. I have faint memories of occasional

visits to my grandparents' lair at Holland Hall in the year or so after my father left, but a letter written to my mother by a friend in 1961 contains the telling sentence 'I was relieved to know that you still won't let Rupert get mixed up with that rotten lot', which implies some pretty furious thwarting of their attempts to keep contact. When one morning in September 1963 my mother told me that my grandfather Poodah had suddenly died, I felt no sadness at all – he was someone I hadn't seen for aeons, someone whom I had long ago consigned to a buried, irrelevant past.

So I can only guess that a couple of years previously, harsh words had been spoken or a telephone slammed down peremptorily, and the thin cords of civility had snapped. Like Medea, my mother then made us all hers, and for five, six, perhaps even seven years, we did not lay eyes on a single member of the Christiansen family, or at any rate I was unaware of any communication from them beyond Christmas cards. If this deprivation seems cruel – if there is any hint in this of my mother using us as pawns in her campaign – I want to say now in the most emphatic way possible that throughout my childhood, she was an absolutely wonderful mother. Any intuition I have of the selflessness of true love comes from the light she shone on my early years – a light which remains the beacon and lodestar by which everything and everyone else in my life has been judged, as well as the source of whatever moral or emotional stability I possess. But that isn't what I want to write about here.

My mother's rage was the chocolate coating of her mindset; it could melt or solidify, but it was only the visible outer surface of her feelings. Far deeper and tougher to crack was the hard nut of shame, the kernel of what it meant to a woman of that era to be divorced.

By shame, I mean not only a head hung low, but also a fetid miasma of remorse, guilt and embarrassment, kept in circulation by the winds and tides of prevalent social attitudes. Nobody has put it more succinctly than A Alvarez in his book *Life after Marriage*:

> *Neither a sexual revolution nor enlightened legislation can eliminate overnight more than a thousand years of divorce taboo. It lives on like a ghost, chilly and half-perceived, generating a kind of moral shudder even in those to whom religion no longer means much and society does not accuse. Pride, or the superego, takes over where the church and community leave off, and no amount of acceptance or understanding or social indifference lessen the sense of personal failure ...*

A lot of 'ordinary' women may have been divorced

in the mid to late 1940s, but that was because of the war: Hitler provided us with an excuse for making mistakes and the watershed of his defeat gave everyone a clean slate and a chance to start again. Since the early 1950s, however, divorce had become a dirty word again, literally unspoken in polite society (a friend of mine remembers her mother substituting the gesture of passing her index finger swiftly across her throat like a knife and making a scrunching noise: done for, dead meat, hara-kiri). Divorce was the sort of thing only filthy-rich people and ridiculous film starlets did – the Duchess of Bedford, Zsa Zsa Gabor, the Gay Divorcee. Among ordinary folk, it was a notifiable disease, like tuberculosis; of course, it wasn't your fault, but please keep it hidden behind the rhododendrons and don't talk about it in front of the children.

Why were divorced women not allowed to enter the Royal Enclosure at Ascot or take the sacraments, why were they subjected to a scattershot of similar petty prohibitions and humiliations?

Because divorcees were always on the qui vive for another husband and therefore a menace to other marriages! Because they had let the side down: Fifth Columnists sabotaging the consensus and refusing to play the game of being British and middle class and better than anyone else!

Even more pernicious than this sort of abject

reasoning – the gratuitously cruel sprinkle of salt on the wound – was the sneer. A divorced woman may not have been legally to blame if her husband had gone off with another woman and you ought to give the poor thing a consoling pat on the back, but why would he do such a thing? Because she wasn't up to it. Because she couldn't keep him happy in bed. If you know what I mean. If you get the picture, nudge nudge wink wink. Isn't this what Mr Justice Caulfield meant when he leeringly referred to Jeffrey Archer's wife as 'fragrant' in his summing-up of the notorious 1987 libel case? She's a corker and I fancy a bit of a goer, and why on earth would a man with such a fragrant wife on tap want to consort with stinky old prostitutes?

My mother ranked as peculiar, in the same awkward category as the Liberal MP Eric Lubbock, who had won the local constituency off the Conservatives in a sensational by-election in 1962. (The only remark I can remember anyone in Petts Wood ever making about Lubbock is that he wore red socks. This observation wasn't intended to imply covert communistic leanings; what the departure from the norm of black or grey suggested much more forcefully was someone dangerously 'bohemian' in his domestic habits. A knitted tie would have fallen just within the accepted sartorial limit.)

It would be melodramatic to say that she was treated

as a pariah; this was suburban middle England, and people didn't do such things. There was no yellow star or scarlet letter; she wasn't shunned or excluded, just subtly degraded – looked at, talked about, pitied from a distance and by tacit agreement marked down as a danger area.

Only occasionally did anyone overtly remind her of her failure to meet the requirements for full club membership. After the divorce, for instance, the unspeakably stupid vicar of St Francis' came round to commiserate and let slip that of course while she would be welcome at the church, the view of the diocesan bishop bla-bla-bla was that she could not take communion or – ahem! – belong to the Mothers' Union. Get knotted. My mother's Christianity was largely superstitious, but after this she would never step foot in St Francis's again, and even now when its attitudes have changed radically, I am not sure I can forgive the C of E for such unChrist-like crassness.

The school run was the conduit for gossip, an intimate environment where parents subtly inter-rogated their defenceless passengers and coaxed us innocents into the unwitting betrayal of confidences and the exposure of concealed truths. 'I hear your mother is playing the guitar,' said foxy Mrs Hinton one day. There was the hint of a curled lip in her tone, implying that this was just the sort of ridicu-lous stunt that could be expected of such a wayward person. It was the first I had heard of a guitar: Ma verged on the tone-deaf, but being reluctant to admit ignorance, I replied, rather cleverly: 'She's thinking about it.' I had learnt to become adept at covering up.

Subsequently it emerged that my infant sister's mispronunciation was to blame. On her school run, what she had actually let slip was the rather less outré news that my mother had catarrh – information which I feel was wilfully misheard and mangled to suit Petts Wood's darker ends. No doubt this particular round of Chinese whispers ended by putting it about that my mother was about to join the Rolling Stones and appear on *Ready, Steady, Go*.

Exhausted by a baby and a four-year-old boy, banged up in an emotionally muffled environment that depressed and antagonised her, my mother did at first struggle. From behind a closed door, I remember anxiously listening to her talking on the telephone to her solicitor, I suppose, or perhaps an intimate friend and sensing a more urgent quality, a higher pitch, in her speech from the one I normally heard – because her continence in front of us children was nothing short of heroic. I only saw her weeping twice, both times silently, without sobbing, and for no apparent reason: once when she was driving down the M1 after a weekend spent at her brother's – he must have said something brutally insensitive that she had been brooding on – and once, with no other context that I can recall, when we were walking back from a shopping expedition together. On both occasions, I asked her what the matter was, but she only mutely shook her head. I must have been eight or nine, and I was frightened – her fear always became my fear, however bravely she repressed it.

Materially speaking, we were not on the breadline. We were lucky to have a bakelite telephone (party line), a vacuum cleaner and a motor car, but life in 1960 had still not delivered the gamut of liberating mod cons. The one-click washing machine and dishwasher were a long way off, the immersion heater was erratic and gas fires ineffectual. In winter, power was cut and pipes froze. There was a lot of hard manual work to be done every day in a middle-class establishment, and it fell to women to do it.

My mother needed help. Her family was scattered – elderly parents in Essex, a married sister in Devon, a widower brother in Nottingham – so she could not call on them, and perhaps she didn't want to, being wounded by their suggestion that she might have been partly to blame for my father's exit. A little on-and-off childcare and perhaps weekly help with the housework from that drone still referred to as a charlady would not have been enough: we needed someone to fill a gap in the family with a fresh injection of love. We needed an au pair girl.

Google does not record the history of this phenomenon, and my researches into the question of whose idea it originally was have proved fruitless. *The Oxford English Dictionary* records a reference in the *Sunday Express* in 1928 to 'a German lady on *au pair* terms to teach German to my children in return for education in English', but my guess is that the element of housework and childcare only entered the arrangement with the post-war 'servant shortage', promoted by some committee for European peace, love and understanding, and chiefly French–English in its axis. Other families we knew looked to Germany, Denmark and Sweden and nowadays you hear of people taking Macedonian boys and I don't know what, but we always stuck to France and seventeen- or eighteen-year-old females, because my mother spoke fair schoolgirl French, knew Paris well and liked what she knew of its inhabitants – brusque, she thought them, but likely to be on the ball and not two-faced.

They came to us through an agency that still seems to run cultural exchange programmes, Le Club des Quatre Vents. The standard length of their sojourn was a year and once they arrived, they either stayed or left: I don't recall any of them ever nipping home for a long weekend or Christmas.

'Au pair' implies equality as well as exchange, but this was not always the case. A lot of girls were treated as little better than housemaids, and a series of lurid newspaper stories – au pair or white slave? – led in the early 1970s to some protective legislation. My mother certainly gave her charges quite a lot of work and responsibility, but apart from their board and lodging, modest pocket money and a day off, they were truly and genuinely made part of our household, included in the party when we went to visit friends or the cinema and never left to feel that they belonged between stairs.

Outside our house, however, they were regarded as the exotics of the neighbourhood, much discussed at coffee mornings and stared at in the street as dangerous incitements to adultery. We scarcely lived in the sticks – Trafalgar Square was half an hour away by train – but at a time when the line for a foreign telephone call had to be booked days in advance and was reserved for dire emergencies, before the entente of the Common Market and the proliferation of package holidays and charter flights in the later 1960s, France seemed a long way off and anyone hailing from *La Ville Lumière* was worthy of note and perhaps a wide berth too.

A complete list of these creatures would be otiose, and in any case several of them I can recall only hazily. In middle age they flow in a Proustian parade through my memory, *jeunes filles en fleurs*, all bearing like the muses some emblem or insignia of themselves, but at times evanescing into each other so that I cannot tell which was which. Françoise, a leggy and limpid beauty, with a great beehive of blonde hair and weekly subscriptions to *Elle* and *Marie Claire*, a being who belonged in the rue Faubourg Saint-Honoré rather than Station Square, Petts Wood. The merry little *piaf* Annie, the benignly imperturbable Denise, the intense and musical Patricia, who had a forehead covered with acne and played the hell out of the easier Chopin preludes on our cottage piano. Or stolid, solid Dominique, who suddenly wilted and ran back to Paris in tears over an unsuspected *affaire de coeur*. Or whimsical breastless Sylvie, who wore a fluffy angora cardigan, pleated mini-skirt and long white socks and could have walked into or out of a film by Eric Rohmer. I think there was a Nadine too, from Saint-Etienne, but Anna has no recollection of a girl with any such name and thinks that I have dreamt her existence.

I could well be confused. Too young to be a surrogate mother, too old to be a convincing elder sister, possessed of indeterminate authority and power over me, they were very confusing – not least because I felt so much for each of them when they were there, so little shortly after they had gone. For Ma, the more intelligent ones were a lifeline, and not just because of their help with housework and childcare. With one of them, Nicole Tisserand, she had a special bond which I have never quite understood. Nicole, known as Coggie, was with us around 1960-61, the period in which the divorce was being negotiated. When Nicole arrived, she admitted to my mother that like the troubled Antoine in Truffaut's autobiographical film *Les quatre cents coups*, she had hit back at her battering or molesting or neglectful parents and been sent to some sort of reform school, where I have a vague sense from a later conversation with my mother that she was caught up in lesbian intrigues. The au pair agency had not mentioned any of this when presenting her as a candidate and initially Ma was alarmed at putting a delinquent in loco parentis. But greatly to her credit and against all the proprieties of Petts Wood, she decided that she liked the girl and would keep her.

She went on to feed Coggie the emotional stability she needed, while Coggie for her part became my mother's confidante and a mainstay through some of her rockiest moments. The evidence of this rests on a few letters from Coggie, written after her return to France, in which my mother is addressed as 'Dear old Mummy Oxo' and reference is made to an accident that my father had suffered – 'I felt sorry for you when I heard that Michael had an accident, because I knew you couldn't help feeling sorry for him' – and scorn is poured on 'the King', my grandfather Arthur, and news of his participation in the film *The*

Day the Earth Caught Fire – 'I am so sorry I can't see it, for it would have given me a real laugh'.

(While researching this book, I was excited to discover through the internet that one Nicole Tisserand had translated Anita Brookner's novels into French. This felt right to me – she was clearly someone of high intelligence as well as an exceptional mastery of idiomatic English – and a hazy mugshot image of her on a website suggested that she could be our Coggie. I attempted to trace her, in the hope that she could provide me with crucial information about this otherwise unrecorded period, but the trail ran cold and I received no response.)

The sort of intimate support that I believe Coggie provided was not easy to come by locally: people in Petts Wood just didn't like divorced women, and my mother retaliated crisply by making it clear that she didn't like Petts Wood people either. Not so much a chip on her shoulder, one might say, as a bleeding chunk gouged out of it. Of course, there were exceptions, women with some imagination and compassion; we were not friendless, just adrift in a hostile environment. And there was also the awful business, still an inevitable feature of divorce, whereby friends have to choose which party to side with. For my mother, the cruellest cut came from Pat C. She was my mother's soul mate, herself a former Fleet Street hack confined to a semi-detached in South

Norwood, with two children roughly the same ages as Anna and me. We spent several Christmas Days there and even as a seven- or eight-year-old, I remember thinking that Pat could be my mother's sister, so closely did they share the same dry sense of humour, based in a general impatience with the folly of the world. But Pat's husband was a crime reporter, and when he landed a plum job on the *Sunday Mirror* under my father's editorship, the temperature dropped and relations were virtually severed. My mother was deeply hurt by this betrayal, which remained unresolved.

In London, my mother had her staunchest allies in a fascinating and powerful upper-middle-class clan, generally known as the Salmons and the Glucksteins, whose family tree spreads its branches as far as Margaret Thatcher's guru Sir Keith Joseph and the celebrity cook Nigella Lawson.

Thoroughly assimilated, with a solid fortune rooted in the J Lyons empire (tea shops and corner houses, groceries, including Lyons Maid ice cream, and the catering contract for Buckingham Palace), the Salmons and Glucksteins were the Jewish equivalent of Galsworthy's Forsytes and as a breed kind, sensible, amusing, liberal-minded and cultured. They sat on committees and contributed to charities, but the ones I knew were without any sort of sanctimoniousness. My mother had been drawn into

My hand clasping my mother's hand, a gesture of
mutual protectiveness and collusion. Anna smiles
in the lap of Anne-Christine, our most go-go au
pair, who married an English art student

their circle through her affection for a colleague at
the *Daily Mail* called Cynthia Gluckstein, who had
died young from leukaemia. Her bereaved parents,
Ros and Dore, who had also lost their son in the war,
subsequently embraced Cynthia's close friends to
help them keep her memory alive. My mother valued

Ros and Dore's wisdom and warmth, and looked to them rather than her own parents for good counsel. They and their siblings and cousins – a strongly inter-married network – became a bulwark against the pettiness of Petts Wood and suggested to me another model of how an un-nuclear family might operate.

So much for the grown-ups, who reacted to my mother's strong personality both positively and negatively. The young, even in Petts Wood, always saw her differently. Boys being by nature conventional and lovers of the norm, my schoolfriends tended to regard her as strange and disconcertingly interesting. The girls, however, were unequivocal: it would not be hyperbolic to say that they were infatuated. What they sensed was a freer spirit: they responded to her gaiety, beauty and glamour, and they relished her indolent indifference to the puritan codes of housewifery that held their parents prisoner.

Let me give one example. Over the road was the McPhee family, our staunch reliable neighbours, always ready to help out and never prone to interfere. In Petts Wood's terms, they had migrated from the lower-middle-class tuppenny side of the tracks, but they commanded respect from even the sixpenny snobs. Father John had been a prisoner-of-war and now worked as an exhibitions organiser; mother Joyce was something to do with the Girl Guides and must have had sleeves embroidered with every badge in the Baden-Powell book. In their resource-fully furnished, scrubbed and polished house, she was never idle: she cooked, she gardened, she sewed and knitted, she banged nails into walls and hung out washing, she erected tents and repaired machinery, she attended the Congregational church on Sundays, and generally made the most of very little in the way of money or material luxuries.

She also brought up four excellent daughters, Anne, Fionna, Alison and Katy, supplementing their ordinary state education with elocution and ballet classes. The daily lives of the McPhee girls were run on rotas, and through that discipline they were going to better themselves, which indeed they did. So to them, my mother represented a more easeful existence, one in which women did not always toil and spin. The normal rules did not apply.

'Kay had the confidence that came from her class,' my sister's bosom friend Katy remembers, 'the sort of confidence that allows you to believe that by divine right you will not get run over whilst crossing even if you don't look both ways. She seemed fearless, with a razor-sharp wit and her impersonations were always spot-on. Even if you hadn't met their victims, it didn't matter, she made everyone laugh. Although I was a little bit terrified of her – she could spot my Achilles heel a mile off – I loved being in your house because everything was so different. In our home, everything was always bustling with people of the Girl Guide persuasion. Her housewifely skills were eccentric. Meals were thrown together, cushion covers glued together with Copydex. Yet she was always stylish. Dressed impeccably, she reminded me of Barbara Goalen [a famous model of the 1950s] – tall, elegant and the whole look topped off with constant cigarettes, sometimes smoked through a holder.'

Fionna recalls her 'afternoon naps, her painted nails, pearl earrings and black velvet hair-band and hair-piece, and her total impracticality. She would often ask my father to rescue her from some small domestic impasse – once she knocked on the front door to ask him to change a light bulb while he was still shaving. I watched her try to thread a needle hampered by her long nails, and realised that she had never learnt to sew or had any interest in doing so'.

Tragically, the McPhee family imploded when its linch-pin, mother Joyce, died from cancer while three of the children were still at school and father John broke down and vanished. For Alison, my mother was 'incredibly understanding when this was happening and always there for us, a huge support'. Fionna agrees: 'She came over and told me that I should not dwell on the last few years when their lives fell apart but to think further back to happier memories.' Katy lived with us for some time before briefly emigrating to New Zealand to live with her eldest sister Anne; when she returned to England, she came to regard my mother as a surrogate parent. The McPhees' story seems at this point much more tragic than my own.

And what the girls' memories remind me forcefully is that I must not paint my mother as someone flattened by her divorce: bloodied but unbowed would be the more accurate description. One of her favourite novels was Elizabeth Jenkins' *The Tortoise and the Hare*, which tells the sad story of how the gentle beautiful maternal Imogen watches helplessly and loses all self-esteem as her lawyer husband becomes infatuated with Blanche, a plain, blunt, huntin' and shootin' woman of no obvious charms. Although she previously considered herself blissfully happy, Imogen does not fight back: she takes it all meekly, almost as though she feels she must have deserved the humiliation. I suppose Ma identified with Imogen, but she could hardly have been less like her. My father had knocked her down, but she was not out. She went back to work, and there would be other men in her life.

Work first. My father's presence effectively put barriers up against her re-entry to Fleet Street and newspapers, so instead she launched herself as a freelance journalist, operating mostly off a manual

typewriter on the dining-room table and contrib-
uting 'the woman's angle' to various magazines,
notably a car monthly in which she wrote a regular
column, test-driving the latest models. This was a
source of some hilarity among those who knew her,
as she was an atrocious driver, constantly scrunching
the gears and forgetting to signal, blithely indifferent
to the Highway Code and shamelessly ignorant of
anything that went on under the bonnet.

She also became one of a band of women touring
department stores and demonstrating to the staff
the wonders of Du Pont's man-made fibres such as
Orlon, Lycra and Corfam. This sounds as though it
must have been terribly boring. It might have been
more fun making a television advertisement– thanks
to a friend she had in the business – for Blue Band
margarine, in which she was filmed as a 'real' house-
wife hymning the virtues of this repellent synthetic
product as she spread it straight from the fridge on
to a piece of bread and handed it to my smiling little
sister.

The slogan which came up on the screen at the
end asserted: 'Mrs Christiansen always uses Blue
Band'. (Oh no, she didn't.) 'We saw your mother on
the television last night,' said Mrs Hinton, fixing her
gimlet stare on me via the car mirror on the school
run, and failing to conceal that curled-lip sneer which
implied that there was something lamentably vulgar

about such a performance.

In the mid-1960s, with both of us children in full-time schooling, Ma began to work in London in public relations, then a new and burgeoning service industry based on ideas drawn from the US marketing mavens. A lot of her old Fleet Street muckers had also hitched themselves to this bandwagon, and for a time she flourished, working on accounts ranging from the launch of the 'revolutionary' Scholl exercise sandal to British American Tobacco, in the course of which she travelled throughout Europe as well as to New York, Brazil, Ghana and Australia. Nowadays this may not seem so very remarkable, but to Petts Wood ladies of this era, the idea of an unaccompanied woman constantly criss-crossing the planet on business was bizarre to the point of being reprehensible. 'Where is your mother going next?' asked Mrs Hinton, who took the same holiday every year in Budleigh Salterton. 'The moon?' she might have added.

I can imagine Mrs Hinton speculating about the boyfriends too. I got to meet an amiable egghead of a rocket scientist called Thoby Fisher and a slimy spiv of an Italian called Clelio Moretti. I don't think either of them cut much ice or reached first base, but who knows? There were probably others too, with whom I imagine she flirted harmlessly over lunch in discreet restaurants, but only one of these admirers was of any significance in her life, and I count the failure of their relationship as the most disastrous fallout from the divorce. He was a man of some allure and stature: our very own Don Draper, had we but known it, our little taste of the sleek New York of the *Mad Men* era. He could have transformed our lives, saved and redeemed us, and he came within an ace of doing so. This is as much of the story as I can reassemble.

He was an American maritime lawyer called John Sheneman, partner in a prominent Manhattan firm called Zock, Petrie, Sheneman and Reid. Tall and burly with thinning, greying hair, he wore the classic American wardrobe of the era: Brooks Brothers suits, button-collared white shirts, penny loafers and infinitely long black socks. Educated at Harvard, he had in the mid-1950s been a member of an expedition to locate the north magnetic pole. Now in his forties, he was divorced without children, and lived at the Harvard Club in midtown Manhattan. Business seemed to bring him to London regularly in the early sixties, and it was at a party given by some scion of the Salmons and the Glucksteins that he and my mother met.

He was much nicer and less introverted than Don Draper – warm, funny, good-tempered and considerate. My mother couldn't have done better, and they fell deeply in love, of that I am sure: children understand such things without the words or the experience to explain their intuition, and I knew that my mother was suddenly happier, that John was the protector we needed and the father figure we lacked. He never threatened to become the alienating step-parent, and never made me feel that he wanted to take my mother away from me.

He managed to be at the same time intoxicatingly strange – I had never met an American before – and entirely familiar. I kissed him on the cheek when seeing him after an absence and cuddled up to him on the sofa – in our more tactile era, one can have no idea of the significance of this (and I know few of my eight- or nine-year-old friends would have been so close to their fathers). I roared with laughter when some idiocy provoked him to his catch-phrase, 'Spare me that', uttered with a comically melodramatic roll of the eyes. We could have made a family: one beautiful memory I have is of the four of us on the sofa together somnolently listening to Beethoven's 'Pastoral' Symphony after supper. John's arms embracing us, his feet stretched out on the coffee table as the storm of the fourth movement abated and the Shepherds' song brought the sun out again.

In front of Anna and me, the lovers were restrained. Whenever he stayed the night, John slept on the sofa, and although I once heard kissing through a closed door, I never saw them in any sort of clinch, let alone in bed together. Whenever he was in town, she would absent herself for a couple of nights, leaving us with the au pair girl of the moment, the pay-off coming in terms of a binge of a weekend treat.

Because John was fabulously generous, in the lavish money-no-object style for which Americans are legendary. On every transatlantic visit, he brought with him presents which seemed to tumble out of his pockets, just for fun, often in fairy-tale quantities – a hundred bars of Cadbury's milk chocolate, a gross of HB pencils (and I am not exaggerating). But this was just the casual small change: he gave with more measured sensitivity too.

Uncles and godfathers were always trying to toughen me up with boy-scout stuff, but John had the grace to accept me the way I was. And because he knew I was hopelessly stage-struck, he regularly brought me a stack of LPs of the latest Broadway musicals (their legacy being a totally futile recall of the scores of such mid-sixties duds as *Carnival*, *I Had a Ball* and *Baker Street*, as well as encounters with the likes of *Fiddler on the Roof* and *Funny Girl* before they hit the West End). Nor do I forget Sheldon Cheney's splendid tome *The Theatre: Three Thousand Years of Drama, Acting and Stagecraft*, or a £10 note (something I had never seen before), an Enicar watch and a Moulton bicycle.

On Anna he bestowed, among much else, what she called her 'Paris dress', a darling blue-and-white checked thing with low flapper-era pleats that was the booty from a trip with my mother to the George V, a set of Joan Walsh Anglund's twee but enchanting 'Love' homilies and a copy of the first edition of Maurice Sendak's *Where the Wild Things Are* (which would now be worth thousands if only she hadn't scribbled on it in biro and torn the cover).

Another aspect of his munificence was lunch at one of the grand hotels at which he was staying – temples of old-school mahogany luxury such as Claridge's, the Savoy, the Connaught and the Ritz, as well as the dazzling chrome halls of the Carlton Tower on Sloane Street and the Hilton in Park Lane, where a rooftop restaurant offered a thrillingly transgressive view into the gardens of Buckingham Palace. Steak and chips was my preferred choice from the menu, with roast chicken (then a relative rarity) a close second.

After lunch came the heaven of the show. If I have never seen the film of *The Sound of Music*, that is because by the time it was released, I had experienced the higher bliss of seeing the stage version from a box at the Palace Theatre, courtesy of John. In the interval, he summoned the usher, whispered something in his ear and pressed a pound note into his hand – the result being that at the end of the

I KNOW YOU'RE GOING TO BE HAPPY

performance I was taken to the stage door to meet no less a personage than Maria von Trapp herself, a young actress called Jean Bayliss. 'I was told that someone wants to meet me,' she said as she emerged, somewhat baffled, in dressing gown and make-up. I was gently pushed forward and rose to the occasion, untying my tongue to tell her that I thought she was awfully good. She smilingly autographed my programme and waved us goodbye. This was altogether an event of giddying wondrousness which took me as near to Nirvana as my young life had yet reached.

On Sundays we went out of London too, for carvery lunches in vast Edwardian country-house hotels in wooded parts of the Home Counties, all of them now a single scumbled blur in my memory. Only twice, however, did we stay out of town, when we went *en famille* for weekends at the Royal Norfolk in Bognor Regis, of all co-respondent places, and the Metropole in Brighton. The au pair girl Coggie, Anna and I were put together in one room and I remember wondering where my mother was sleeping, because she had insisted that if anything untoward occurred in the night, we should consult Coggie.

I can't work out a precise timetable for all this. My impression, as I mentioned, is that he came over at something like three-monthly intervals, probably between 1961 and 1967: certainly the last present I recall receiving from him was that of four stalls for *The Magic Flute* at Covent Garden in January 1968. But it's possible that the visits were irregular, and I wonder now if they split up at some point and then got back together again.

In any case, his absences brought a steady flow of letters. In those days, when postmen called first thing, I would take the morning drop up to Ma in bed along with a pot of tea, and every day brought a thick white envelope, marked at the top-left-hand corner either Zock, Petrie, Sheneman and Reid or the Harvard Club, and addressed in John's round, large, sloping hand to Kate Christiansen – in itself a marker, as everyone else called her Kay, a diminutive of Kathleen that she loathed. What went on inside the envelopes, however, remained a mystery: all I ever determined was that the contents were generally of one page. In reading them, my mother betrayed no emotion. And I was never once aware of her writing back to him.

Some years later, left alone in the house, I ignored injunctions to respect a lady's privacy (looking inside my mother's handbag would have been a betrayal to match the breaking of a promise) and discovered shoeboxes full of these letters, kept on a shelf at the top of her wardrobe. Two of these survived – why? – a cull she must have made later in life:

My beloved

Not one wink did I sleep last night – I dozed and a moment later I was awake – loving, longing and fretting about you.

Believe me, my treasure, I love you with all my heart

———————————

My darling, my darling

I really do not believe I can go on much longer without seeing you. You occupy my every thought – not a moment goes by that's not devoted to you. How love can be so wonderful and yet leave me so desperately lonely – is beyond all comprehension …

I dream of your meeting me at the airport – and then dashing away to a lovely English village where I could hold you close and tell you how much I miss need and love you. …

Do you really know how I love you – and how much – and how every moment without you is an eternity?

Stumbling on something so intensely intimate made my cheeks flush hot red, and I never again felt any temptation to explore the boxes further. I plead guilty to this day for prying, and even now, long after their deaths, I feel ambivalent about exposing such private emotion. But I would like to know why my mother never married a man whom she loved and who loved her and who could have been our saviour from everything we hated about a straitened suburban existence.

This is my only conclusion. John's generosity to me and Anna was bountiful enough, but in relation to my mother it overflowed: he must have offered her whatever she wanted materially, which wouldn't have been obscenely much. Suddenly her wardrobe was full of soft and silken items with labels like Bergdorf Goodman, and her dressing table was graced with the scent of Carven Ma Griffe, the notes of which ('aldehydes, gardenia, asafoetida, clary sage and citruses') brought her instantly back to life when I took a whiff from a sample bottle in Peter Jones the other day.

Books too. I don't think Ma ever bought a book for herself. She read thoughtfully and copiously, but she was entirely reliant on the public library or Christmas presents and even when I was studying literature at university, she continued to regard my casual purchase of paperbacks as reprehensible extravagance. The shelves in the sitting room were in consequence very static, their contents serving quite literally as wallpaper – and although I was hungry for certain sorts of reading matter from an early age, neither the likes of *The Aerodrome* by Rex

Warner nor the *Memoirs of Field Marshal Montgomery*
appealed. What is the use of a book without pictures
or conversations? Alice wisely asks herself. Or one
that doesn't focus on a gang of rollicking pre-adoles-
cents, I might have added.

But John brought novelties: at least there was
something different to look at, as room was found
for Allen Drury's *Advise and Consent*, Gore Vidal's
Julian, Arthur M Schlesinger's *A Thousand Days*
and Mary McCarthy's *The Group*. I guess from this
list that he was a Democrat, a JFK man, a liberal
progressive, but I cannot recall him ever talking
about Communism, Civil Rights, Vietnam or any of
the great issues of the day. What did we talk about,
now I come to think about it?

If you are ten, as I was thereabouts, you tend
to take what's offered without thinking about the
moral quagmire of indebtedness into which you are
wading. For my mother, it was different, and there
came a point when she felt she could accept no more.
A birthday present, during his absence, came out of
the blue as a brand-new Triumph Herald. She sent
it back to the dealer – a gesture which suggests to
me not so much self-respect as cold feet. There must
have been a broader problem: I can only guess John
had asked her to marry him and she had refused; I
can only guess that she did not want to uproot us
and move to New York, and that after my married-

HARVARD CLUB
27 WEST 44TH STREET

Tuesday 5pm

My beloved,

not one wink did I sleep last night – I dozed and a moment later I was awake – loving, worrying and fretting about you.

Believe me, my treasure – I love you with all my heart. JR

to-the-job father, she could not countenance another absentee husband. Even deeper than that, I think that my father's betrayal hadn't so much rattled her confidence as shattered it: she could never trust anyone again, even herself.

But unless I am totally mistaken in my estimation of his integrity and there was something that I didn't know or someone else involved, I can't help thinking that she made a big mistake. This was one of those crucial moments in life at which one should take a risk on saying yes rather than playing safe and saying no. Anna and I were perfectly ready to emigrate: in fact, we talked about it excitedly when playing together, basing our fantasies on a book by Enid Blyton in which an ordinary family sails the Atlantic on a luxury liner. My mother's ties to her family and friends weren't so close that she would have withered at a distance from them. In the US, there would have been a high chance of a better, happier life for all of us. We knew another family in Orpington who had gone to live in Scarsdale and loved it. But without John, we were doomed to more of the same, and that in the end is what we got.

So our very own Don Draper disappeared from view. Sending back the Triumph Herald marks an end to the story. I never thought to ask Ma what had happened to him, perhaps because my own life had moved into the solipsism of adolescence, and John was seldom mentioned again, except as distant history. Early on in the affair, she had asked my sister and me not to discuss him with other people, and gradually I realised that very few of her friends knew anything about it. I remember being quite hurt when she irritably insisted that sometimes she needed a bit of 'life for herself', even from her children – surely, as her first-born I had a divine right to round-the-clock access – but now I feel deeply sympathetic to her reticence, especially as I guess that for a long time she was havering over the relationship and didn't want pressure on a decision from any external quarter. Would she now object to my attempt at an exhumation? Perhaps. One photograph survived of the two of them together: sitting on deckchairs on a shingle beach, wearing conspiratorial dark glasses, they looked suspiciously at my camera. After my mother died, we carefully mounted the snap into an album of family pictures. Unaccountably, it has recently vanished.

———————

Now I must pause in her story. It is time to rewind the tape, move to the other side of the courtroom and attempt to imagine it from my father's angle. Imagining it is all I can do: for this version of the story, I don't have many bricks of fact to build on, and no personal experience. I've talked about him and his life to people who knew him professionally, and garnered from surviving relations a few relevant anecdotes and resonant remarks. But there are huge gaps in my knowledge, and what follows can only rank as guesswork – I cannot pretend otherwise.

She was driving him crazy, and a nervous four-year-old and a screaming baby drove him closer to the edge. He nodded in wry agreement at Cyril Connolly's celebrated maxim that 'the greatest enemy of good art' – for which read successful journalism – 'was the pram in the hall'. She nagged him, she needled him, she bullied him: she was more ambitious for him than he was for himself, or rather she wanted him to achieve what he wanted via a path that he did not wish to take. The obvious comparison with the marital psychology of the Macbeths presents itself: 'What thou wouldst highly, that thou wouldst holily,' Lady M muses on her vacillating husband: she would prefer him to take the short cut. My mother's professional morality was pragmatic: poverty and principles go together, she would say cynically. She didn't believe it in her private life – where she was one of the most stubbornly principled people I have ever met – but she had an embattled sense of the world out there being a hard, cold place in which everyone had to fight their own corner and nurture their own interests. There was a touch of Ayn Rand in this, I have to admit, and I don't think that among her generation it was at all uncommon.

He wanted to have fun and mess around, acting the jovial eccentric and playing cricket on a Sunday.

She wanted him to be tough, decisive, straight as a die, financially prudent and home on time— and also provide her with more domestic support. He saw her point, but that wasn't who he was. She was worn down, he was worn down, and suddenly they could not renew each other and the tank of love was empty. Simple as that.

And there she was: the other woman. Not a flame-haired temptress, not pouting Marilyn Monroe or smouldering Jane Russell perhaps, but someone in her twenties ready and poised and sexually heated whose antennae had quickly sensed an unhappy marriage and a querulous wife. She was prepared to make that seediest of transgressions: taking another woman's husband. She fixed her sights and fired.

Christina Robinson was generally known as Chris. She came from Wimbledon where she initially worked on a local paper. After providing the *Sunday Pictorial* with a good tip-off, she asked for a job there and was made secretary to my father, at that time the paper's assistant editor with particular responsibility for the night shift.

'She was one pushy broad,' Tony Miles remembers. 'Cropped hair, saucy and provocative.' Men were generally charmed, but other women at the *Mirror* firmly disliked her, according to her former colleague the fashion editor Felicity Green. 'I couldn't bear her,' she told me. 'I knew what her game was instantly. She made outrageous play for your father, and didn't bother to hide it. Everyone in the office knew what was going on, long before it came out. And then one morning she came in and actually said: "I got him between the sheets last night".'

Christina was not her first name: she was christened Alice Christina Vera Ellen. But by dropping Alice and jumping to the name by which my grandfather was also known, she allowed my father to marry his father and perhaps disentangle that psychologically intricate knot with which he struggled. I don't know if she made the alteration on arriving at the *Mirror*, but even if it serendipitously preceded this event, it looks like one hell of a cunningly prescient move.

I'm guessing now, guessing wildly: this is what you have to do in a memoir, because after 50 years nobody remembers more than the bare facts. But I can imagine that La Chris said that she would do it all for him. She would understand what he needed – the space and freedom to do his job, the boozy camaraderie and the fun of the late-night poker. She wouldn't mind about his pet stuffed alligator, which my mother had refused to have in the house and which ended up on a shelf in his office. She could see the joke, she wasn't a spoilsport! She wasn't interested in being a wife calling him to order, no sirree! Instead she'd be more like a bosom pal, at his side but never dragging him one way or another.

She became pregnant. At this point, he had to choose between her siren call and my mother's prosaic Reality Principle. The latter was something he had never been so keen on: brought up in an atmosphere of wealth and privilege, with a father whose dazzling career demonstrated how dreams could come true in the midst of a family which airily felt its fate to lie above that of the common herd. He wasn't good at being decisive. He felt loyalty to his wife, and loved his children, but in the end he had to think about what was best for his own life and career. So he chose La Chris. Her baby, incidentally, never came to parturition.

Guessing, I'm still guessing. Through the painful period of separation and divorce (on the grounds of adultery, in 1962), my mother's behaviour was understandably hysterical and vengeful. My father was often profoundly upset by her vituperation, and shocked by the iron curtain that she prohibitively drew around my sister and myself. Gently and insidiously, like Belial in *Paradise Lost*, La Chris persuaded him that the best way to calm her down was to give her sole custody of the children and to renounce all claim to their affections. Total divorce from his old life, a complete and clean break, bar the alimony. A heavy price, but wasn't it ultimately for the best of all parties? Give her what she wanted, let her get on with it – wouldn't that be the way to help her to accept, to move on?

They could start their own family together – and now certifiable facts begin to surface again. A daughter was born in 1963, a son a couple of years later. She gave up work to look after them and they moved from Earl's Court to a house in suburban Essex.

Sometimes, however, she would appear in the office. After the first edition of the paper went down to the printers, it was traditional for senior management to break off and open a self-congratulatory bottle or two. Wives and girlfriends often participated in this ritual, which La Chris particularly enjoyed. Increasingly, however, people noticed that her drinking was becoming compulsive and embarrassing. 'She seemed slightly mad and deluded at times, spinning fantasies that she had been a model for Dior,' *Mirror* journalist Mike Molloy recalls. 'I'd say she was borderline alcoholic.'

Meanwhile my father's career was booming. In 1963, Cecil King, the *Mirror*'s patrician proprietor, appointed him the first editor of the *Sunday Mirror*, a re-launch of the *Sunday Pictorial*. My father had a bold vision for the title: it would be a new sort of tabloid, one which would toss aside grumpy cloth-cap socialism and stop relying on the toxically addictive combination of salacious sexiness and grime

crime. Instead it would feel lighter, cleaner, clev-
erer, fresher, funnier, faster, younger – reflecting the
easing of the moral stays after the Lady Chatterley
ruling and the spirit of youth and change ushered
in by the Beatles and Bond, Julie Christie and Tom
Courtenay, espresso bars and Vespa scooters. The
North was coming down South, and new voices were
clamouring to be heard. We hadn't quite reached
Swinging London yet, but the *Sunday Mirror* would
help us get there.

There was a significant change of design and type-
face – out went the aggressively plain and masculine
Kreiner Condensed, in came the less assertive, more
forgiving Placard. Some great scoops and exposés
were pulled off, the first being the discovery of 'The
Little White Room,' a tiny rented flat in Wapping
that was the secret love nest of Tony Armstrong-
Jones and his then girlfriend Princess Margaret. The
whole thing was handled tactfully, and no offence
taken: when the couple married, Armstrong-Jones
became Lord Snowdon and his photographs regularly appeared in the paper. Serialising Desmond
Morris's trailblazing study of human behavioural
patterns *The Naked Ape* (the rights purchased at
the then considerable cost of £10,000) was another
huge and daring coup which boosted circulation
and precipitated a new vogue for popular science.
Nakedness also sold copies when in 1966 the *Sunday*

Mirror became the first newspaper to print a picture of a female nude, tastefully photographed by the fashionable sixties portraitist Shahrokh Hatami: the inevitable complaint to the Press Council was not upheld, on the grounds that the image was artistic rather than prurient in intent.

My father's qualities as an editor were legion. Mike Molloy pays tribute to him as 'the most complete all-round journalist I ever knew. There wasn't a part of the newspaper that he couldn't deal with – sport, features, news, layout. He was a natural leader, with a big, generous personality which made him very popular. He kept morale high, he made you feel good. He loved the fun of it all – getting togged up for Ascot, riotous Sunday cricket matches which all the staff had to attend, an annual booze-up day trip to Calais.' Tony Miles agrees. 'He had a rumbustious quality and loved the hurly-burly of newspapers. He also had flair, and a capacity to think outside the box. Never boring, always kind and astonishingly patient – he never bawled anyone out, which in newspapers is rare indeed.'

There was one problem: it was perfectly clear that he had a screw loose. 'Quite considerably bonkers' is how Felicity Green puts it. 'He had bees in his bonnet which left some of us worrying about his sanity.' Out of office hours, this characteristic manifested itself in harmless fashion. He wrote the lyrics for a song, for example, which was published and recorded by an old-time Temperance Seven sort of an outfit called Bob Wallis's Storyville Jazzmen – a rather dreary, stoned dirge, which suggests that he slummed it in drinking holes of a rather lower class than El Vino's:

We've 'ad yer money Mister
You've 'ad yer moments Mate
Come along, come along
Come along, come along please

Ain'tcher got no 'ome ter go to?
Gettin' awful late
'Urry up 'urry up, 'urry up
'Urry up please

At home, he also indulged a penchant for amateur dramatics, a hobby which he did not take altogether seriously. Mike Molloy remembers witnessing his church-hall performance as the eponymous Inspector in JB Priestley's *An Inspector Calls*, in which he wore 'a ludicrous very false beard and flailed about, hamming it up and clutching his head to buy himself time as he desperately tried to remember his lines. A whole party of *Mirror* journalists were dragooned into attending and we sat there sobbing with laughter.'

But in the office this streak of anarchy became increasingly dangerous to someone in his position, threatening his authority and alarming his superiors. The *Mirror* columnist Christopher Ward describes him as being 'like a great conductor who stands on the podium before the orchestra one morning, drops his baton and says "Bugger Beethoven, let's boogie."' Felicity Green remembers walking into his office one morning and screaming at what she saw. 'Your father lay flat on the floor with a golf ball on his forehead. Standing above him was his chum the assistant editor Cyril Kersh, swinging a club as though he was about to tee off.' His Maoist wheeze that everyone should go topsy-turvy and swap jobs for a week caused terrific consternation: the thundering columnist Cassandra, otherwise William Connor, was not amused at the proposal that he might find it fun to assume briefly the mantle of gardening correspondent. 'Mike,' he quipped brilliantly, 'you are a marshmallow masquerading as a ping-pong ball.' Another columnist, Quentin Crewe, was told that he could write about 'butterflies, the habits of elvers, aspects of the French Revolution or speculations on the nature of pithecanthropus'. Crewe took him up on the offer, and they became fast friends.

In his autobiography, the distinguished foreign correspondent John Pilger remembers being interviewed as a rookie by my father for his first job at the *Mirror*:

As he entered his office he leapt at me, gripping an arm and bellowing 'You're just what we want, an Australian!'

He explained that although winter was almost upon us, a final and crucial game of cricket was to be played against the Daily Express the following Saturday ... 'And what do you do best, Pilger?'

'I bowl,' I said, 'I spin bowl.'

'Splendid ... you start on the Mirror tomorrow.'

'What as?' I enquired

'Oh, we'll work that out ...'

Such casual tomfoolery was always doomed to hit the buffers eventually, and when it did the collision was fatal. In the eyes of his immediate superior Hugh Cudlipp – the *Daily Mirror*'s former editor and now the group's chairman following the retirement of Cecil King – he had gone too far and he had to be stopped. Mike Molloy explains that 'to hit the jackpot in newspapers you had to have the backing of the boss upstairs. Larry Lamb had it with Murdoch at the *Sun*, Harold Evans had it with Lord Thomson at the *Sunday Times* – and Arthur Christiansen had supremely had it with Lord Beaverbrook. Your father had a good relationship with Cecil King who protected him and enjoyed his company, but Cudlipp was a much trickier customer – a bully and a windbag who had worked his way out from the Welsh valleys and got most of his education in pubs.

He was unnerved by upper-middle-class people like your father and disliked what he saw as their airs and graces.'

Following some humiliatingly public insults, Cudlipp formally dressed my father down in 1971 by means of an acerbic and unambiguous sixteen-page confidential memo, which my father kept and later discreetly allowed other people in Cudlipp's firing line to see. 'You know I have not been happy about the *Sunday Mirror* for some time,' it began bluntly. After detailing the drop in sales – up to over five million in 1967–9, it was down half a million by 1971 – he then proceeds to lash out. Too much opinion and too many columnists, not enough narrative and adventure. Looking over his shoulder at Murdoch and realising that he was about to sharpen and sensationalise the *Sun* and *News of the World*, Cudlipp accuses the *Sunday Mirror* of being needlessly 'ESOTERIC', that is, 'communicated to, or intelligible by, the initiated only'.

> *So far as the wider audience is concerned – even if they have heard L'Après-midi d'un faune – have they heard of Debussy or can they pronounce his name? ... How many of our readers have heard of Stanley Spencer, or have the slightest notion what his religious-cum-sexmania murals are all about? ... On a different level, you already know my views*

*on the series about 'Was God an Astronaut?' and
the sacred mushroom etc. I have yet to meet, frankly,
any 1970 or 1971 dolly girl or modern young man
who is likely to be impressed by the phallic qualities
of the sacred mushroom.*

He then proceeds to demand changes of personnel,
singling out Quentin Crewe and his elvers for special
excoriation:

*Until you thin out some of the deadwood you can't
take on new talent, and that is what the paper
urgently needs ...*

before concluding with an ex cathedra order:

*Re-tune the contents to maximum popular appeal
– but still retaining strong opinion on serious socio-
logical, industrial and political affairs.*

*Plunge with enthusiasm into investigatory jour-
nalism. Why can't we get exposures like the Sunday
Times's revelations on the time-coding of food for
human consumption or the Daily Mirror's disclo-
sures on jerry-built houses? Let us steal the initia-
tive immediately in this field – it would do the paper
a power of good.*

This may have been good horse-sense but at a
personal level it was a devastating infringement of
his editorial independence and nothing less than a

vote of no-confidence; unable to capitulate to such a blatant demand for a total volte-face in his policy and judgment, he lost heart. A few months later, using a further decline in circulation to back his position, Cudlipp called him in for the inevitable ultimatum. 'I can either fire you, or you can go to the *Daily Mirror* as deputy editor,' he said – either way it was a demotion, not least as the *Daily Mirror*'s editor Tony Miles was younger and a former *Sunday Mirror* subordinate. Bravely or cravenly, he chose the latter option.

The move could have been a disaster, but my father wasn't arrogant and he buckled down. Once the dust had settled, he and Miles got on very well and when Miles was summoned upstairs in 1974, he did not resent my father being given his job. Cudlipp had by this point retired as chairman and the new top brass, led by Edward Pickering – a Christiansen family friend and my useless godfather – was canny enough to measure my father's positive qualities (his energy and inventiveness, his popularity with the staff) against the negative ones (his whimsicality and want of Arthur Christiansen's instinct for the tastes and thoughts of the ordinary working man). Perhaps they felt that the memo's rap across the knuckles had had the desired effect of bringing him to his senses, or perhaps there was just no other obvious candidate for the job. So at the age of 47, my father achieved his ambition to edit a national daily newspaper. Before the inexorable rise of Murdoch's the *Sun*, the *Daily Mirror* then boasted the biggest circulation in Fleet Street, and at last my father could now feel that he stood alongside his father rather than in his shadow.

———————

Stop and rewind again. There is yet another side of the story – one which I can tell rather more authoritatively, simply because it is my own.

While that photographer flashed and snapped on the day that my father announced his departure, I lay on the floor with my chin resting on my hands and watched the Sunday afternoon BBC classic serial on the television: my preoccupied gaze is clear from a few of the surviving images, one of which appears on the dust jacket of this book. Something about something called the Wars of the Roses was being broadcast. Being not quite five, I can barely have understood it. Yet I vividly remember being powerfully drawn – with an intensity that I can only interpret now as erotically charged – to a young man on the screen wearing a black tunic and tights.

Over the years, I came to think of this as what a psychoanalyst would call a false memory – a retrospective construct, painted in much later than the original canvas. But the *Radio Time*s of July and August 1959 informs me that there was indeed such a 5.35pm serial, called *The Golden Spur*, 'a tale of

the Wars of the Roses by Constance Cox', in which
the cast included young Oliver Reed as Richard of
Gloucester and someone called Edward Vaughan-
Scott as the teenage hero Tom Fenton. (My guess
is that my love-object was the latter; I have always
been drawn to the name Tom.)

Can this be the source of my homosexual orien-
tation? Can the human psyche turn on its axis and
reboot so suddenly? Had I overheard my father
telling my mother that afternoon that he was leaving
– had I heard quarrelling and tears, had I sensed
anguish and catastrophe? – and did I begin then
and there my quest for a substitute? I am inclined
to answer yes to all these questions, Dr Freud, even
though the little boy in those photographs doesn't
look as though anything was unduly bothering him.
Well, Dante fell for Beatrice when they were eight or
nine; perhaps I just beat them to it.

After this, I remember so little, and none of it in
any discernible order. The lights come on only when
I go to my nice prep school at the age of eight and
begin to develop an identity. Trying to recover those
lost four years is like staring at a table randomly
covered with pieces of a very complicated jigsaw. I
stare at the incoherent mess for hours and occasionally I can fit a tiny section together. But there is no
way I can make overall sense of it.

Before my father left, I remember him and another

man erecting a swing in the back garden on the occasion of my birthday. I remember being taken to see him in his office, where he sat in a glass-framed cubby hole with a typewriter on a desk. I remember the ailing of my budgerigar, which my mother told me came to a grisly climax after my father had the wheeze of feeding it medicinal brandy down a pipette.

I remember a holiday in Alassio, during what must have been the summer of 1958, when my mother was halfway through her second pregnancy. I would have been almost four. I remember sitting and lying in the back of the car – a galumphing great roaring spluttering beast of an Alvis, my mother later told me, which repeatedly broke down or overheated on the long, slow journey through France before the *autoroutes*. I remember what fun I had covertly digging my fingers into the torn seams on the ribbed leather seats and picking at the raw white stuffing underneath. I remember the rough whitewashed exterior of the rented villa, and an outside stairwell leading to a flat roof where we ate breakfast. I remember the sweet and faintly rotten smell of the squishy figs in the garden, and a related infantile ditty presumably extemporised by my father to commemorate some lavatorial contretemps:

If you eat some figgies
You will do some biggies

I remember the horridness of heated sterilised milk and picking off the creepy filmy skin that formed over it. I remember the plump smiling maid Luisa who petted me and pinched my cheeks, turning the un-Italian name of Rupert into *Roberto, cheechee Roberto*, and I remember chanting with her my first words of Italian, *caldo e freddo*. I remember the *caldo* sand beneath my bare feet on the long beach and even the taste of *freddo* orange ice cream.

All small sensory memories of no significance. But they have an unreal oneiric quality, and somehow my father's actual physical presence is altogether absent in them, as though his features have been airbrushed out and only his outline left in blank silhouette.

Nor can I remember the timbre of his voice, or any emotion attached to his absence or presence. I cannot remember either his arrival filling me with joy or his departure searing me with pain. I cannot remember his touch, I cannot remember talking to him. I have trawled every lane and alley throughout the teeming city of my memory, I have dredged and scraped the bran tub and shaken the empty bottle through sleepless nights and long walks, and still nothing comes, nothing stirs or beckons. It is as though I have locked a granite door and thrown away the only key, or dragged a sealing slab of immovable marble across the entry to the tomb, leaving the mummified – daddified – corpse and its treasures to rot and gather dust within. 'Rub him out of the roll call and drum him out of your dreams', as Nellie Forbush sings as she tries to wash that man right out of her hair in *South Pacific*. I did as she advises.

Perhaps I went even further. Children, so we are told by the psychologists and pundits, tend to blame themselves for the collapse of their parents' marriages, and this is a prime source of their subsequent personality disorders. I suspect there is some sentimentality in this view, and it certainly doesn't fit my case. Along Oedipal lines, I simply decided to kill my father – but not so much out of jealousy of his relationship with my mother, as in revenge for the way he abandoned me (just as in the myth, Laius initially betrays his son and forfeits his loyalty by putting him out on a hillside to die as a baby). If you think this is a bit fanciful, then at least consider the evidence that children do not think in terms of compassion, exoneration or pardon: until they are educated otherwise, their world consists of themselves and their own interests and appetites. Nothing so ruthless or cold-hearted as a child: they can murder without compunction or a sense of consequence.

So inside my head I did the deed, and it worked wonders. The only time I again felt any significant emotion relating to my father was when his sister, my aunt, told me that he was 'very proud' that I had won a scholarship to Cambridge. This enraged me to the point of mephitic fury. Proud of me, or proud of himself for having a son thus honoured? How dare he be proud of me? What the hell had he to do with it?

Children were told very little in those days; they were permitted little continuity with the adult world; truth was thought to be something better concealed and even lied about if convenient. We were left to draw our own conclusions, as when a nice little girl at my nursery school simply vanished one day and never came back. She had died from polio, but that is only something I gathered years later. 'Don't ask questions: curiosity killed the cat.' Hilary Mantel touches on this in her astonishing autobiography *Giving up the Ghost*.

Much of what happened to you, in your early life, was constructed inside your head. You were a passive observer, you were the done-to, you were the not-explained-to; you had to listen at doors for information, or sometimes it was what you overheard; but just as often it was disinformation, or half a tale, and much of the time you probably put the wrong construction on what you picked up. How then can you create a narrative of your own life?

I don't think of this as a malign conspiracy to keep children in the dark. The opposite, in fact: behind it was a sincere and urgent desire to keep us in the light, sparing us the possible pain and guilt of experience. Good parents left their offspring in a state of Edenic innocence as long as possible, encouraged them to believe in Father Christmas and dream of the world as a kindly U-certificate place where Enid Blyton's idea of fun set the tone, and God had numbered every hair of your head and made all things bright and beautiful. The liberalism of Dr Spock's gentle advice on childcare fed into this, and perhaps the memory of the war too: forgive our parents, they have had their fill of death.

My father never called or wrote. Sometimes he remembered my birthday and sometimes he didn't, likewise Christmas: it is the unreliability that seems so reprehensibly cruel to me now. You should not let a child down like that: a child needs consistency from a parent almost as much as he needs love – for what is professed love without its envelope of trust? An old friend of my mother's told me that she remembers coming to lunch and offering to buy me some scrapbooks for the cuttings and souvenirs I obsessively accrued at the age of seven or eight. At the end of her visit, she said: 'I have this vivid memory of you looking up at me pleadingly. "You won't forget about the scrapbooks will you, Pat? Because Daddy always does." It was one of the saddest things I have ever heard from a child.'

I hope this doesn't sound mawkishly self-pitying.

After all, other people gave me presents on cue, twice a year. But I have to say that the last gift I received from my father – which constituted my very last communication with him of any description – appeared so monumentally crass as to be wilfully cruel, and for many years I puzzled over what could have motivated it.

For my eleventh birthday in 1965, he sent me a razor – the Gillette Techmatic model, the novelty of the year. Having not even approached the stubble of puberty, I still had the glabrous chin of a new-born baby and no need of such an instrument: indeed, living as I did in such a female environment, I knew nothing of the craft of shaving. I remember staring at this inexplicable weapon, this arcane gadget, with a mixture of despair and bafflement. A message from Daddy: what did it mean?

My mother was enraged on my behalf. She helped me to negotiate a refund from Gillette (something that, with her passion for just reparation of every penny that was rightfully hers, she was very good at), but I also wonder if she wrote to my father about his gaffe with such venom that her wrath became a pretext for dropping the whole idea of sending presents at all. In any case, nothing else ever appeared.

But as I was researching this memoir, I was granted one of those small but serendipitous revelations that life in its mysterious grace occasionally delivers. Browsing through that remarkable stash of letters that my father wrote home while he was evacuated in America, something jumped out and made my heart thump. It is dated February 1941, when my father was still thirteen. 'The shaving so far has been moderate,' he tells his father. 'Once every three weeks I cut off the rapidly stiffening stubble. The razor is a beauty, a Gillette, and there is no shortage of blades.' It was clearly a sensitive issue.

Then, in April 1942, he reported that for his fifteenth birthday, he had received from his younger sister 'twenty razor blades, as I had used up my first packet of Gillette blades'.

'My son will never be advised not to shave,' he continued, 'providing he has something worth cutting off. I have now been shaving for sixteen months, and I still only have to shave every two weeks, whereas one would imagine from the pre-razor period that I would be getting up ten minutes earlier every morning to shave stiff bristles by now.'

So there it was: what had seemed like indifference or callousness was intended as a blessing – a clumsy attempt at a father-and-son thing, a misguided, remotely controlled push through a rite of passage which finally made sense to me after nearly half a century.

The first surviving evidence of my literary bent comes from a faded copy of my prep-school magazine, where in 1964 REN Christiansen aged ten took a bow and presented his verdict of the epic movie *Cleopatra*, which he had been taken to see at the Dominion, Tottenham Court Road.

I reproduce this wretchedly uninspired and unimaginative debut to provide some light relief and also to demonstrate how anyone displaying a wafer-thin veneer of bogus sophistication and absolutely no early sign of critical acumen or stylistic elegance (let alone intellectual precocity or a finely tuned ear for English prose) can somehow end up making a respectable career out of writing and hold down the position I have now held for sixteen years – that of opera critic of a distinguished broadsheet national newspaper.

I saw Cleopatra, a great film, yesterday. Elizabeth Taylor acted authentically, although she was not as commanding a personality as she should have been. Mark Antony was played very well in some parts, in others he was just 'him'. This role was played by Richard Burton.

Rex Harrison's Caesar was a dream come true. Hume Cronyil [sic] as Sosigenes was absolutely 'lousy'. Pamela Brown played the High Priestess very well.

The settings were marvellous, three being most notable, the Roman forum, Cleopatra's barge and the Egyptian forum. Irene Sharaff designed Elizabeth's costumes as have never been seen before. Xittorio Novarasee [sic] brought brilliance into the men's costumes while Joseph Manciewicz proved himself to be one of the greatest directors of the day [as if I knew anything about the others.]

Although this film was basically a spectacle, there was a great deal of good acting. But I do not think Cleopatra was perfect (no film ever is!). There are a thousand and one details that would take too long to discuss.

What does shine through this dismal 3-out-of-10 effort is someone with an idea of being something in the world, someone with hopes of being listened to and making his mark. Is that me there? And to be more specific, is there a trace here of the same nitwit bravado that marked my father's wartime letters home?

My psychic root, however, was a sense of a secret status which nobody else shared – or if they did they kept jolly quiet about it. I didn't know of anyone in Petts Wood, nor of anyone at my prep school, whose parents were divorced. I was never clear whether this was a mark of distinction or an obscure disgrace, but it certainly wasn't something I discussed. 'Don't talk about our personal affairs,' my mother would say crisply, and we didn't. A little frisson of fear shook me when I thought about the possible consequences of classified information leaking out in the wrong quarters, whatever they might be. My sister circumnavigated the problem in even brisker fashion: she simply told everyone that her father was dead.

From there, however, I moved on to the comforting fantasy that I was singled out, and déclassé. I have always been spellbound by those heroes of nineteenth-century novels who can be described as the Young Men in a Hurry – Stendhal's Julien Sorel and Balzac's Lucien Rubempré, for example, poor provincial youths who want to make it in the big city. Of this breed, Pip Pirrip in *Great Expectations* is closest to my heart, and I believe that Dickens identified himself very closely with this character, who narrates the entire novel in the first person.

Most readers misunderstand him, however, or rather take him at his own valuation of himself, which is an unduly low one. His voice implies someone remarkably couth, intelligent and sensitive, yet someone who feels burdened by a failure to live up to a moral ideal. Throughout the tale, he flagellates his younger self mercilessly for his worldly infatuation with glamour and his trivial dream of becoming a fashionable young blade. As he looks

back in maturity after a professional career spent
working solidly in a trading company out in the east,
he tells us moreover that he feels he was a heel for
accepting the escape he was magically offered and
deserting Joe's forge. He should have stayed there
and married the girl next door.

The temptation to concur with this sanctimo-
nious Victorian moralising should be resisted. My
reading of the situation is that Pip did the right thing
in taking the money: he was too smart and savvy to
end up as a blacksmith in a village on the marshes, so
he got out and tried to make the best of himself. (The
source of the cash is irrelevant, as he wasn't allowed
to know from whom it emanated and had every
reason to believe that it was someone 'respectable'.)
Of course he wanted to be in with the in-crowd, of
course he wanted fun, of course he craved an environment denser with interest, variety and adventure
than the one marked by what Karl Marx called 'the
idiocy of village life'. Pip was young, for heaven's
sake, and young people do tend to get a bit rowdy
and drink too much.

Anyway, I knew how Pip felt – how the young Pip
felt, that is, not the Pip who narrates the novel and
berates himself for not being primly high-minded
and renunciatory. Like young Pip, I craved elegance
and sophistication: I wanted to live in Alan Bennett's
house in Gloucester Crescent NW1 and mix with an

upper-middle-class intelligentsia who valued culture above straight behaviour. I felt that I belonged with them, and that my membership of this élite had been denied to me by my mother's divorce.

Call me a snob, if you like; I don't care: but it wasn't the snobbery of despising other people so much as the snobbery of a romance of myself, at the back of which was the contrast between our modest suburban estate and both the knowledge that the name of Christiansen had some cachet in the wide world and the memory of the glittering baubles which John Sheneman had bestowed. It may not have been the noblest path to self-improvement, but I don't think it was altogether venal.

There were several way-stations along this road, the first being my prep-school art teacher Diana Fenwick. She and her husband and three children (in whom I was uninterested) lived a faintly bohemian existence embodying the fag end of Bloomsbury enlightenment. They were saturated in Third Programme culture: they knew nothing about *Steptoe and Son* or the Who, because their lodestars were Henry Moore and Bernard Leach and TS Eliot and Benjamin Britten. They took their holidays in St Ives or Portmeirion, where they walked for miles across windswept moors and grilled sausages on barbecues on deserted beaches. At home, they smoked untipped cigarettes, listened to Mozart operas and Monteverdi madrigals, wore Fair Isle pullovers, polka-dotted kerchiefs, berets and sandals, lit wood fires and made things – their own clothes, papier-mâché models, Elizabeth David's ragoûts and bouillabaisses for their earthenware pots. Stains, dirt and grease did not faze them, creature comforts concerned them little. They were out-moded modernists, fading out around 1955 – Pop Art and brutalism and John Osborne weren't on their radar. America was bad, France was good, and they didn't care for Harold Wilson or the white heat of technology. To me, they were free spirits, breathing pure ozone.

One evening in the school holidays, Diana invited me to supper. The rest of her family was away on holiday: she had stayed at home to work at her kiln and paint some blobby Ivon Hitchensy canvases. It was just the two of us. She told me about her years at Dartington Hall and art school and her ambitions for her pots and painting, and then she asked me what I wanted from life and what I thought about things. I do not think for a moment that anything erotic was in the air, but it was infatuating: I was twelve and it seemed like the first time anyone had taken me seriously. After we had eaten something with a French name off dinner plates which she had herself made and painted, she played me her gramophone records of *Le Nozze di Figaro*, which we followed with the vocal score. What a night – an epoch in my life, a

Damascene moment. New vistas had opened up, and I saw the world in different colours and heard another song being sung. I wafted home with an airy spring in my step and Mozart in my heart: I had found my religion.

Then a sharp tug pulled me back to Planet Petts Wood, where only half-pint measures of aesthetic enthusiasm were licensed. I opened the front door twenty minutes later than I had agreed, and saw my mother looking down at me from the top of the stairs. She said nothing: there was no tirade, no recrimination, but the rueful reproach in her gaze scalded me. It was as though I had betrayed her, abandoned her, joined up with an obscure renegade enemy. And so I had: I had found something to replace her and her dreams, and from that moment our bond would slacken and weaken. It never recovered its tautness or strength, and I must now live out my days with the regrets entailed.

It must have been only months later that I was sent to Millfield, a maverick public school in the West Country best known for the enormous range of sporting facilities it offered and therefore generally considered wildly inappropriate for someone artistic in temperament who had absolutely no wish to take advantage of a diving platform, judo hall or squash court. But the place had other attractions too: it was fully co-educational, which at that time was still very uncommon; it gave everyone an individually tailored timetable; and it was fuelled on the Robin Hood principle that anybody accepted should pay only what they could afford, this last being crucial to my mother's decision to send me there. She could afford £30 a term, or so she successfully argued: I guess the offspring of the likes of Elizabeth Taylor or the King of Thailand or Bin Laden *père* were subsidising me ten times ten.

I didn't like it there much. Gratitude didn't enter my calculations, and in my Pippish way, I considered the tone of the place *arriviste* and a bit vulgar (which it was), dreamily imagining that I would have shone brighter at Westminster or Bryanston. But despite my total lack of enthusiasm on the games front, I tried to make the best of it, and thanks to a couple of splendid and encouraging teachers, I eventually won a scholarship to King's College, Cambridge. After postgraduate study in New York, I dropped the idea of becoming a literary academic and had a brief and mediocre career in publishing. In 1982 I decided to follow the path of least resistance and became a freelance journalist, specialising in the arts and eventually focusing on opera and ballet. I had never intended to enter the ancestral profession – in fact I had felt positively hostile towards it – but what else was I good for? I have done all right, and certainly don't feel cheated. But that's enough about me.

My father was only allowed to sit in the editor's swiv-elling leather chair and enjoy the view from his pent-house suite for a pathetically short period.

Despite Cudlipp's injunctions to lay off the funny stuff he had introduced into the *Sunday Mirror*, he started by refusing to play his new brief straight or to quell his old buccaneering bravado. Most auda-cious of all was a plan to stake out a fresh and more outward-looking approach by commissioning a vastly expensive series of supplements, exploring, embracing and engaging with our new friends in the Common Market, a body which Britain had only just joined. So only three months into his tenure he was based in Paris, supervising the paper's splashy praise of the cuisine, culture and dazzle of Pompidou's post-Gaullist regime and its enterprisingly expansionist esprit. Perhaps there was a thing or two we could learn from the Frogs after all.

The impulse was generous and sincere, but this was politically controversial territory, and given the ambivalence of the paper's core readership towards Europe, not an obviously circulation-boosting strategy. Edward Pickering had given my father his head at first, but told him that he must take full responsibility for his whims and as soon as it became plain that the whole idea was backfiring, he was sharply summoned back to London. Even though I doubt that the sack would have been administered at such an early stage of his tenure, his blood pressure must have risen in anticipation of a nasty carpeting.

En route home by car, he stopped at a hotel in Boulogne. Waking in the middle of the night, he reached out for a glass of water and suffered a stroke which paralysed one arm. He was only 48, but that is an age that would now be considered dangerously elderly for a job as stressful as that of editor of a national newspaper. Before the clean-living era of dawn jogging with executive personal trainers, he was also considerably overweight, as well as an uninhibited drinker and persistent smoker whose nearest approach to healthy exercise was the trot between the two creases of Kentish village-green cricket pitches on a summer Sunday afternoon.

Driven by a colleague but without consulting any sort of doctor, he came straight back into the office the next morning to face the music. He passed through that hoop of fire unscathed, but the cardiac specialist he saw later insisted that it would be suicidal to do anything less than resign immediately.

Mike Molloy took over and would serve with distinction as editor for a decade. At a farewell launch in the Connaught Rooms, my father barely kept his composure as he described to a gathering of the Fleet Street great and not-so-good how he had spent 30-odd years climbing to the top of the greasy pole, but fate had decided not to allow him to perch there. Hugh Cudlipp wrote him a perfectly decent but scarcely effusive letter (are there sardonically gritted teeth in front of the adverbs 'completely' and 'successfully'?) expressing his regret.

> *All I can say is that it is absolutely lousy luck that illness prevented you from having a good long run as editor of the* Daily Mirror. *Obviously it would have been daft to have tried to carry on in the circumstances, but that does not completely compensate one for having to put up with the intervention of the Almighty in affairs which are no business of his at all, such as the editorship of the* Daily Mirror.*
>
> *Nevertheless you have had a great career in Fleet Street and very successfully held the really big jobs at the top, including your time at the* Daily Mail. *Jodi joins me in sending you and Chris our best wishes.*

There was, however, a brief attempt to find my father something less taxing to do within the Mirror Group. According to his friend and *Mirror* colleague Tony Delano, he was sent to the US,

> *ostensibly to study some new production system at a plant in North Carolina (or somewhere). I took*

*delivery of him in New York and later drove him
down to Washington or wherever it was. He spent
a fortnight or so there, which bought London some
time. It was a distressing experience. He was, I
imagine, on heavy sedatives which on top of the
stroke left him a shadow of his earlier self. He had
lost much weight. He had hardly any conversation
and showed little response to anything or anyone.
All his old enthusiasm and boisterousness had
gone. My girlfriend of the time. a Washington Post
reporter, was reduced to tears. 'That poor man ...
just waiting to die.'*

Perhaps he rallied a bit, but there was no way that
he could be kept on in a dignified position.

*We've 'ad yer money Mister
You've 'ad yer moments Mate*

He retired to his suburban close near Chelmsford,
and passes out of the historical record via some snide
paragraphs which appeared in *Private Eye* in 1977.

They are not long, the days of wine and roses.
*Michael Christiansen, 50, who edited the Daily
Mirror for less than a year before suffering a stroke
and being dismissed, now runs a second-hand book-
stall in Chelmsford market.*
*Son of the legendary Chris who made the Daily
Express, Mike pays £9.60 for his barrow. His wares*

the other day included such significant tomes as
Books for Thinking People, Sexual Adventure in
Marriage and Etiquette Properly Explained.

PS Mike is thought to have received a £75,000
golden handshake from the Mirror when he made
way for Boy Wonder Mike Molloy...

Huh. I read this when I had just taken a double
First at Cambridge and won a Fulbright scholarship
to study at Columbia University. Huh. It was my
turn to clasp the top of the greasy pole, and in ruthless Pippish fashion, I remember feeling or thinking
nothing at this turn of events except faint embarrassment at being associated with someone who had
sunk so low. So life went on, and I heard nothing
more and cared nothing either.

But seven years later, I had duly slipped down the
pole a little myself. Through the bleak years of the
Falklands War and the miners' strike, I was sharing
a flat with a friend from university as I struggled to
write my first book and earn some money as a freelance journalist and jack of all literary trades. One
summer evening, I was in the middle of marking
what seemed like a bottomless pile of A-level English
papers – soul-destroying work – when the phone
rang. It was my mother, sounding distraught, to tell
me that my father had died: having suffered another
stroke while driving, he had crashed into a wall and

killed himself. I told her that I would come over to see her the following day.

In another room, I could hear my flatmate and her sister laughing about something. It was one of those moments when one is dissociated by shock from the reality of the world, but the sensation did not last very long – within a minute or two, I had joined the girls, successfully pretending for the rest of the evening that nothing had happened.

My mother was calm but understandably rattled. We decided that it would be undignified and contentious to attend the funeral, but that I should send some flowers. I called Interflora, and suddenly realised that I did not know what to write on the card accompanying the wreath. Love and best wishes? Sorry I never got round to calling? So you got your come-uppance, you heartless bastard? And how should I address him across eternity – as Daddy, Dad, Pa, Pop, my father, Mike? I knew I had no picture of him, but I had not realised that I had no name for him either. Who was he to me? My unease was not alleviated by the death notice correctly but pointedly inserted in *The Times*:

CHRISTIANSEN – on Tuesday June 12th, suddenly, Michael Robin, beloved husband of Christina, elder son of Brenda and the late Arthur Christiansen, much loved father of Rufus and Sarah

*and father of Rupert and Anna. Funeral service
at 1pm, Danbury Parish Church, Essex. Family
flowers only.*

It was hardly an olive branch.

Nor did my mother behave tactfully by writing
over-promptly to Christina to enquire about a life
insurance policy of which we would be the benefi-
ciaries. An understandably savage letter was fired
back, written in exquisite calligraphic script: yes, she
believed there would be £2,500 for each of us, but
couldn't my mother have left off until the obsequies
were decently complete? I couldn't help but agree
with her. The money eventually came – at least he
had kept up the payments – and it provided enough
for me to put a deposit on my first flat. Thank you.

My mother also sent her condolences to the
dreaded Brenda, who had already lost her younger
son Andrew to alcoholism and heart failure. Or
rather, I have a copy of a letter that she may or may
not have sent to a former mother-in-law who had not
been kind to her. It must have been very painful to
write, but the more often I read it, the more double-
edged it seems – on the one hand, honest yet tactful;
on the other, almost gloating with a barely repressed
sense of ultimate triumph.

I am so sad, particularly for you and all the terrible

*blows you have had to take with such courage. It
takes a long time for death to sink in and to realise
that someone has gone for ever. On the plus side, I
suppose we can say that if he had survived he might
have been paralysed and equally that although his
life was not very long I think he enjoyed it to the full
and in the last years was able to relax and play a lot
of golf and cricket which he loved.*

    *I shared my youth with him and there are many
very happy memories. Lovely hols in Paris and Italy
with the sun shining and when we first fell in love the
whole world seemed to be singing for me.*

'The whole world seemed to be singing for me'
– I find those words unbearably sad and painfully
beautiful.

*It's funny the odd memories that come flooding in. I
remember Hollocks [the chauffeur] letting him drive
the car one night (no licence). And do you remember
coming to dinner one night and he'd been to the
fishmonger and bought an entire slab of ice for the
drinks? He was an eccentric creature and very sensitive inside … What a rotten old world. I have no
idea what it's all about but I hope that he will rest in
peace and meet his father again.*

We read the obituaries with interest, no more.
Although I could sense my mother reflecting on
it all and softening her attitude, we never visited

the grave – to this day, I don't know where it is – and we also absented ourselves from the memorial service. Yet out of long pent-up anger and recent grief Christina would launch one last murderous attack which suggests that her hatred of my mother was every bit as intense as my mother's hatred of her. God, however, was at this point on our side.

One day, a few months after my father's death, Anna went round to my mother's flat on some small errand. My mother was out at work, and the place was empty. While she was there, the doorbell rang and the postman delivered a parcel addressed to my mother. Anna noted that the postmark was Chelmsford, where my father had lived, and telephoned me with her suspicion that it had been sent by Christina.

We decided that we ought to open it, and I rushed over to the flat in the car. It was indeed as Anna had thought. The package explained itself through a covering note, written in that same impeccably controlled calligraphic script and reading (I paraphrase, in the absence of the original document): 'I had a very happy marriage to Michael, marred only by your greed and vindictiveness, the evidence of which I now return to you. Yours sincerely, Christina Christiansen.' Then, between some rubber bands, were about 200 letters, still in their envelopes, written to my father. Almost all of them dated from

1959–61 but they were still explosively charged across a quarter of a century, the great majority of them from my mother, but several of them written by me, aged five or six.

The messages from my mother were of two kinds: pleas – terrible, urgent, impassioned pleas, written in blood and tears and despair – to my father to come to his senses and return to his family; and pleas for small amounts of money to cover repairs to the car or a new pair of shoes, alongside formal correspondence from solicitors.

What came from me, in a large, hesitant yet deliberate hand, each word painstakingly composed in pencil along ruled lines, had another sort of poignancy, bleak and monosyllabic. 'Dear Daddy, Please come home. I miss you. Love from Rupert.' My memory wasn't jogged – these were words which came from my period of mental whiteout – but what intrigues me now is that he didn't find these pleas so laceratingly and incriminatingly painful that he crumpled them up and threw them as far away as he could. Instead they must have been filed away somewhere – in a drawer or a folder marked First Marriage/First Child/Divorce perhaps – as though he masochistically didn't quite want to forget the misery he had wrought.

Anyway, we read these letters with our hands shaking and our hearts pounding. Some of them made me sob, some of them I simply could not read. Anna felt the same. We agreed that they should be burnt and felt profound relief at the miraculous chance of being there to receive the parcel. Had it been delivered into my mother's hands, I sincerely believe its venom might have killed her: Glauce turning the tables on Medea.

So we took the letters to the incinerator at the back of the garden and set fire to the lot. Standing hand in hand like frightened, burdened, abandoned children in a Grimm fairy tale, we watched them scorch, flame and carbonise into smoke and ash. A wicked deed had been foiled.

(The only significant postscript to this thread of the story is that I never met my half-brother, who died young, and apart from an encounter of a few seconds at my grandmother Brenda's funeral, I had never met my half-sister either, until I was researching this memoir in 2012. Having established contact via a cousin, we sat down for ten minutes over a cup of coffee near her office in the City. It transpired that she lives with her husband only a few stone throws away from me in south-west London and that we might well have been passing each other's trolleys in the supermarket for years. But I don't think either of us would have felt a magnetic attraction and even now I am not sure I would instantly recognise her again: there was no resemblance I could intuit, and it was as though we had drawn a blank over each other.

I told her that the book would contain material about our father and her mother that she might not find pleasant, and asked her whether there was anything she would like to contribute. In the nicest possible way, she told me that she felt she had nothing to say, but otherwise freely and gracefully licensed me to go ahead with it. I respect her decision and her privacy, but can only add that the sensation of being deep in middle age and coming face to face for the first time with someone who shares half your genes is disconcerting, to say the least.)

By the time she was 50, my mother had lost interest in her career. She grew to hate the increasingly factitious spin of PR in which she was ensnared. She admitted to me once that she yearned to get back to writing, but the moment had passed. There had long been a novel typed up and kept in a cardboard box. One day I realised that it was gone – chucked into a bin or the garden incinerator, and never mentioned again.

Through the seventies and eighties, she dragged on through a series of 'information and communications' jobs in the charity sector that she found increasingly unrewarding, working with people she largely despised. She adored my sister – her rock and mainstay – and her young family, but found me very troublesome and inexplicable. She read widely, enjoyed the theatre and cinema, kept abreast of the news and remained interested in human psychology. But the spark had gone: she had no hope, no faith. Scratchy and crabby, she was quick to take offence where none was intended and I fear that even the staunchest of her diminishing band of friends must sometimes have found her even more irritating than she found them.

It was as though there was a taste of bitter aloes in her saliva, and not even her copious consumption of nicotine and alcohol could wash it out.

She had been pricked by that most subtle yet stinging of emotional insults – the certain knowledge that someone like you has been preferred, that you are just not as good – just not as desirable – as the other is. Nothing, not even the courtly love of that shining knight John Sheneman, could ever heal that raw flesh or its exposed nerve ends; nothing could even soothe or cauterise it into dead scarred tissue. She was hurt by something that went on hurting, and she licked the wound compulsively.

We suffered the fallout from this sensitivity, my sister and I, chiefly in the form of interminable telephone calls during which she droned on about other people's cock-and-bull pretensions and vanities as though they were aggressively directed against her rather than pathetic defensive evidence of their own insecurity, or complained about imagined aspersions cast at her taste, at her cookery, at her garden, at her intellect, at her way of doing things, at her. For God's sake, just ignore them, don't sink to their level, I would say. But like Prometheus bound assailed by vultures, her blood and bile still gushed forth daily.

A more vivid insight into her emotional panic came when I was much older. In 1973, we went to the Royal Court together to see *Not I*, a short play by Samuel Beckett, of whose work and its struggle against the void she always had an instinctive understanding. *Not I* spends fifteen minutes in a woman's mental hell: if she is not quite clinically mad, she is in the vortex of an ultimate disintegration, desperately hanging on to the threads that weave sense into her life. Like staccato Morse code, her thoughts are blurted out:

> *sudden urge to ... tell ... then rush out stop the first she saw ... nearest lavatory ... start pouring it out*

Throughout the agitations of this monologue, all one sees on the otherwise darkened stage is the disembodied voice's sharply illuminated mouth – pink, ululating, labial – and next to it a hooded figure silently bowed in helpless sympathy.

Halfway through this unremitting white-knuckle roller-coaster ride, my mother clutched my arm and dug her fingers in: she was remembering her own tailspin. 'That was me,' was all she could say when it was over. 'I can't bear to talk about it.'

Divorce also exacerbated another of my mother's worst personality traits, a syndrome described somewhere by Henry James as 'the imagination of disaster'. The chief symptom of this was an intense superstitious fear of imminent catastrophe. It was as though she was perched permanently on the edge of a precipice in a headwind, with storms forecast from all directions. If someone was five minutes late, she was seized by visions of them lying bloodied on the road in a fatal accident. If a brown envelope emblazoned with On Her Majesty's Service arrived in the post, it could only contain a ruinous tax demand or a summons to answer an unfounded charge. 'I should *not* like to be a prostitute,' she said with adamantine emphasis while we were watching a television play on the subject, as though some strong arm of the law might arrest her at any moment and deposit her in a brothel. A splutter from the car's exhaust meant a breakdown; every headache would be diagnosed as a brain tumour. The obvious or innocent explanation could not be relied upon, and nothing good could ever be confidently predicted. Her life was wasted in worry.

But another of her defining characteristics served as a counter-weight to this dismally non-Zen philosophy: she was deeply sceptical of authority and refused to be intimidated by any show of it. Her maiden name was Lyon and she lived up to it, being indeed lion-hearted. As a timid, even craven child, I found this aspect of her personality unsettling: so openly scathing was her contempt for policemen, ticket inspectors, customs officers and commissionaires that I lived in dread of her being dragged away and arraigned before the bench for sheer bloody-mindedness.

Now I can I look back and admire her indelible, unquenchable courage, the manifestation of a sturdy yeoman's spirit and its attendant virtues of self-respect and self-reliance. She followed no party line: her vote went to the Conservatives, but only grudgingly and never smugly or unthinkingly so. The world, I feel, could have done with more people like her over the last 250 years, immune to the glamour of utopian masterplans, the rhetoric of Robespierre, the ideologies of Stalin or Hitler. Churchill was her one hero, and she measured every man's worth against his staunch buggering on. In this she was at one, I guess, with her contemporary Margaret Thatcher, who was too close to a type of bossy and humourless Petts Wood woman to be simpatica, but like Winston, someone with whom my mother shared a sincerely romantic belief that Britain's destiny was Great, and that we were freeborn citizens of a morally superior nation in which we never, never shall be slaves. 'This is a damned good country,' she would tell me, and I believed her. That, at least, was the theory, the official line and what you told children; the reality was that the whole thing was being mucked up by lickspittle politicians of the Wilson and Heath eras, who ranked alongside the ticket inspectors and parking wardens as toadies and hypocrites. Only a few cussed back-bench figures of the Gwyneth Dunwoody variety, who spoke their mind and followed their principles whatever their allegiance, squeezed through my mother's needle's eye. They were, come to think of it, people like her.

The sum of it was someone deeply ingrained with the Protestant sense of life as a battleground, a constantly disputed territory in which peace could never break out and allies were not to be trusted. Existentially, one was alone. She was Christian on his Pilgrim's Progress, she was Hamlet taking arms against a sea of troubles, and this made her, at her worst, aggressive, combative and depressive, slashing and burning as she ascribed the worst of motives to blameless people as well as the worst of outcomes to innocent events.

Divorce made the flames flare like a splash of petrol. There could be no settlement while the essential injustice of his desertion stood: on that ground she was black-hearted. She could try and forget, but why should she forgive while she remained the victim and the wound suppurated? The psychology of it is all too obvious. Denied direct revenge on the culprit, she unconsciously took it out on the rest of the world, and on herself.

Fortunately, in the course of this unending strategic campaign, there could be small morale-boosting triumphs against the pompous and prissy. One early opponent was the beaky, tweedy wife of my prep school's headmaster, one Mrs Peggy Lintott, a beast strongly suspected by us boys of peering through the keyhole with a sadistic leer on her face when brutal Major Lintott was administering the whacks in his study.

When I was about nine or ten, this baggage took class music, teaching tonic sol-fa and nobly attempting to awaken our ears by playing us LPs of classical pops. Rightly, she detected some unusual susceptibility in me – I can still remember being transfixed the first time I heard the haunted melancholy waltz in the Prelude to *La Traviata* – and made what I imagine was a responsible and reasonable phone call to my mother, suggesting that I should take piano lessons. But my mother was enraged by such temerity. 'I told that bloody woman that you had enough on your plate at the moment and that she

My mother in her fifties

should mind her own business,' she told me. In this case, however, Mrs Lintott seems to have won, as I soon began studying under Mrs O Fulton FRAM.

But further ructions followed when I became a tearful boarder, and my mother weighed in to dispute the questions of extra exeats, Ancient Greek, permission to wear a vest under my cotton football jersey and the persecution of a gang of bullies in the Remove. Such pleas on my behalf were unsolicited and often caused me extreme embarrassment, as I sensed that Mrs Lintott had identified my mother as a dangerous nuisance and was likely to tar me with the same brush. Too bad – my mother disdained mealy-mouthed tact, preferring to speak bluntly and show her feelings plainly. I know that she had my best interests at heart, and that she simply felt that as my sole parent, her rights over me superseded the school's. But she never realised how her lack of tact jeopardised my fragile sense of security.

After being interviewed by her for the *Daily Mail*, the SOE heroine Odette Sansom told my mother that she would have made an excellent secret agent. She spotted, I suppose, the clarity of focus in her perception of the world and the ruthless determination to achieve her goals, which had made her an exceptionally effective journalist. I can also picture her standing up to the Gestapo, rather as she stood up to officials of any sort, particularly those in peaked caps. A car park attendant who banged his fist on the bonnet of our car when we turned into the wrong bay caused my mother to roll down the window and unleash a tornado of vituperation that would have sent Maria Callas cowering; the man from the gas board who knocked on the door with a piece of paper claiming underpayment of the quarterly account by 4s. 6d. can never have forgotten the Krakatoan tirade that his polite enquiry sparked.

The Ealing comedy element in this – the little

person cocking a salutary snook at those puffed up with vain authority – turned nastier when it came to tradespeople. My mother's attitude to capitalism was in its way as cynical as any Marxist's. Everyone in the system was trying to get as much out of you for as little as possible, so bite or get bitten, trick or be tricked, and watch your back. It was a code consolidated by her experience with my father. She had been gullible, but never again would she be outsmarted.

The most satisfactory vent for this fever was consumer protest. She was mistress of the letter of complaint, and the example I give below shows, I think, an exemplary rhetorical force. Her technique was 100 per cent effective too: the apologies were abject and the refunds came, sometimes with a little extra thrown in.

This, to a mail order firm, is relatively restrained but beautifully succinct and focused:

As it is impossible to reach you via telephone, I am writing to express my extreme indignation at your legally dubious methods of selling and your apparent inability to consult your files – from which you would have discovered that several years ago, I cancelled all my arrangements with you. I owe you nothing and take an extremely dim view of your organisation.

Now you have started to send me unsolicited materials with the proviso that I can send them back

if I do not want them. I shall do no such thing. The
postage costs incurred would be considerable, and I
see no reason why I should pay them. You will send a
carrier to pick them up as soon as possible, and if you
trouble me any further, I shall take legal action.

Copies of such letters were kept in a bulging folder marked AWAITING REPLY. Read en masse, they suggest someone for whom wrath came as naturally as breathing, but this impression would be misleading. It was all a bit of a game, albeit one she played compulsively. She was too morally imaginative and intelligent to be monstrous and the red-hot resentment that she seemed to stoke in her belly didn't only fuel her own cause. After she retired, for instance, she volunteered for the Citizens' Advice Bureau and although she sometimes moaned about the other people she worked with and took a slap-dash attitude to the protocols, she found deep satisfaction in taking up the cudgels on behalf of those who were in real trouble. A Polish woman, slaving as a cleaner in a hospital, who had been fired without due process; a Nigerian family facing eviction; a man looking after his demented wife who couldn't find his way round the benefits system: it wasn't just that, as someone with the soul of a journalist, she was interested by the stories of such people – she felt their situations with a fierce sympathy that went beyond the clichés of sentimental compassion and Welfare State entitlements. Fighting their corner and taking their part, she truly lived up to her maiden name: she was a Lyon, as I have said, and ever lion-hearted.

Many of my friends and contemporaries have divorced, many of them bitterly, a few with the semblance of amity. The curdling of love into hate and respect into contempt remains a horrible, soiling business, and the imagery with which it is regularly described is tellingly savage and gladiatorial. Divorce steals, severs, spits, bleeds. Wolves, rats and vultures! The comedian Robin Williams snarled: 'Ah yes, divorce: from the Latin word, meaning to rip out a man's genitals through his wallet,' while the novelist Margaret Atwood's view is that 'a divorce is like an amputation – you survive it, but there's less of you'. Fiona Shackleton, the lawyer who acted for Prince Charles in terminating his marriage to Diana Spencer, spoke of 'the courtroom as a barbaric venue in which to pick over the carcass of a failed marriage'. I could go on.

But although divorce has become so familiar – just the flip side of marriage, if you like – I don't know of anyone in comparable middle-class peacetime circumstances who did what my father did.

3.

I n the course of writing this memoir and raking over the embers of the past, I have talked to several men of my age group who underwent comparable experiences and tried to find some common ground. (I note with interest that the parents of the new Archbishop of Canterbury, Justin Welby, separated in 1959, the same year as mine: Welby was only two at the time, however. I wonder whether he has any images of the split as bizarre as mine.)

David Kynaston, the only child of an army father and German mother, remembers at the age of eight packing his prep-school trunk at the end of term without any idea of where he would be going:

> *I vaguely knew something was wrong at home, but not what. An aunt eventually came to pick me up, and I was sick in the car. After a week staying with her, during which time I was told nothing, my father came and took me home. He handed me over to my*

mother — that was the last time I ever saw them together — and she took me via the ferry to Bonn, and in a park in front of a statue of Beethoven she told me that she was getting divorced. I don't think I really knew the meaning of the word, but I burst into tears.

From then on, I moved between my father and mother, who had both acquired other partners, at opposite ends of the same village. It was only when I saw a butcher's bill addressed to Mrs K. pinned to the kitchen board in my father's house that I realised he had remarried. I was a religious child, and prayed every night that my father and mother would get back together. For at least ten years I felt so ashamed and embarrassed that I kept the whole situation a deadly secret. I didn't really discuss it with anyone until I was in my thirties and met my wife.

Mark Frith's father was a fighter pilot, while his mother came from a theatrical background:

It was not a love match — they married in 1943, in the trauma of war, and I think that the first years of their marriage were so intense that everything else was downhill. I had four brothers, and we lived in rural Gloucestershire. My father was clearly a serial adulterer and had endless affairs. In 1955 we were told that he was going off to work in America and a taxi thrillingly arrived to take him off to board the Queen Mary. My brothers and I had no idea what was going on, and we went on quite happily living a feral outdoor life in a big house and garden.

My father left in the summer, I remember. At Christmas, I finally asked my mother when he was coming home and she told me that it wasn't certain. At school I concocted stories around the absence of my father which made it seem as though he was still around. It wasn't for another five years or so and the onset of puberty that I realised that he wasn't coming back at all. Sporadically, he sent cards and presents from America, but for twelve or thirteen years after he left, none of us had any real contact.

When I did see him again, I thought he was a rather feeble little man. He came back with his new wife to see his parents — my grandparents, with whom we were in touch. There was a formal tea party on a summer's day and I walked out on to the lawn and there was this man I didn't even recognise and we had a stilted meaningless conversation. I had been excited about meeting him, but he disappointed me — he was unable to rise to the occasion. He wasn't even socially competent. He meant nothing. Was I damaged by all this? Well, aren't we all walking wounded? I just know that my mother was absolutely marvellous throughout.

Alastair Bruton was the youngest of four children

who grew up in the West Country:

> *My parents had been married nearly 20 years in 1964, when I was seven years old, and my father left home to live in London. He later told me that he offered my mother a divorce, but she refused. Instead they pretended that nothing had changed. I was sent off to boarding school which in those days meant that one was safely out of sight for eight months a year. My father would come home for Christmas and Easter and a couple of weekends in the summer, and there was no mention whatsoever of his other life.*
>
> *But of course, children know when something's wrong; they always do. I don't mean that aged ten, I realised that he was living with a younger man; I wasn't capable of admitting that I knew that until I was in my twenties. But from being a perfectly ordinary seven-year-old, without my understanding why, I began to have violent traumas, started running away from school, had to be drugged to get me back there – an intensely difficult period that continued until I was fourteen.*
>
> *Looking back, I can see how awful my parents' situation was. Divorce was bad enough, but homosexuality was inconceivably shameful to people in their world and still criminal. I've often been asked what it was like to have a gay father, but the answer is that my father's sexuality made no difference. Far more painful was his admission, the one and only time that he talked to me openly about his homosexuality, that apart from the*

first two or three years of living with his boyfriend after he left, his life in London had been deeply unhappy.

What I share with these three contemporaries is an element of not knowing, not asking, not feeling – an area of numbed silence. Fifty years on, that territory is filled with a forest of words, and the idea that it is more psychologically healthy to explain these situations patiently and meticulously to even the youngest children is paramount: honesty is seen, in the new jargon, as empowering. The sooner a child loses his or her innocence the better, they say, but perhaps I am rather glad that I kept mine.

Now, as I approach my 60th year, I am left with unanswered questions which afflict me like a flaring itch. How could a civilised, intelligent, sensitive, kind man, free from the grip of alcoholic or narcotic compulsion, not himself abandoned or abused by either his parents or his life, walk away from a four-year-old and a baby?

Whether the way he turned his back on us was his own fully willed and rational decision or the result of a temperamental pusillanimity – or indeed whether my mother had in some respect endorsed or connived at it – must remain a mystery. Had they been asked to explain, I think each would have told you something different.

A second mystery is my own behaviour. The

situation I've been describing has ricocheted aimlessly around the walls of my consciousness for half a century, and the ball never seems to land anywhere or lose it momentum. Why did I so steadfastly refrain from approaching him myself? Nothing positively stopped me, and avenues of contact were open: I could have telephoned him, written to him, sought him out, acknowledged his existence. Loyalty to my mother can only be part of the explanation. Another restraint was – feeble as it may sound – a purely social embarrassment: should we start with an embrace or a handshake, how would one kick the conversation off, what should I call him, what would one say at the end of the encounter – cheerio, nice to have met you after all these years?

The truth is that I simply didn't care: the phrase 'my father' brings no tear to my eye, no burst of anxious adrenalin, no fondly remembered image. The excavation of his past and psychology that I have made in the course of writing this book has stimulated or satisfied my curiosity, but it hasn't aroused any more substantial emotion: it is my mother I feel rawly angry for, and perhaps angry about too.

Today, governments in the UK and elsewhere are moving towards legislation giving divorced fathers more legal right of access to their children – 'a presumption of shared parenting', they call it on the consultation documents – and more responsibility for them. Absent, neglectful fathers who refuse to acknowledge (or turn their backs on) their biological offspring have become a major social problem among the poorer sections of society; conflict also arises when mothers will not allow their ex-husbands near their children, sometimes for fear of kidnap – a phenomenon which has led to the growth of a dubious retaliatory organisation that calls itself Fathers 4 Justice (its use of that numeral rather than the word somehow reducing its credibility). I read about this in the newspapers and think wryly: my people were pioneers here!

The reforms sound so reasonable and humane, 'putting the children first', but I wonder if the resolution can ever be as simple as that. Certainly in my case – a middle-class one, half a century ago, with all that this implies – I feel it was better that we had one home, one parent, one stable set of affections, priorities and domestic rules, one chest of drawers and one view from the bedroom window. I can speak for my sister here too.

We were never caught in the cross-fire and never resorted to the beady manipulations that are the stuff of fictions from Henry James's novel *What Maisie Knew* to Noah Brumbach's film *The Squid and the Whale* (or any of the other 16,000 divorce-related titles apparently available on Amazon). Even if we could not quite know who we were, we knew where we belonged, and in that sense I cannot regard my childhood as a tragedy. Certainly if I turn to the *Mail on Sunday* and read the squalid tug-of-love – tug-of-hate – stories, in which children are virtually kidnapped from their own homes by one or other demented parent, I can even feel not just that we had a lucky escape, but that perhaps there was something noble in the way that my father renounced us.

No, I take that back. As his mother Brenda put it, he failed in honour and the best you can say of him is that he grudgingly paid the price my mother demanded. I don't need to think that he spent the rest of his life silently expiating or at least regretting his sin. It's just as possible that he barely gave it a second thought – he had enough on his plate with another family to manage and a daily newspaper to edit, and latterly the effects of a stroke to negotiate. Life is an onward business, if that's how you choose to take it.

What I do know is that my mother remained the unhappy one, the victim of a moral code which subtly yet cruelly punished the innocent by making them feel inadequate. She bore her divorce like a brand of Cain. She may not have been guilty, but she had failed, which was just as bad. Keep your husband happy was the fifties marital mantra, the pledge that went with the vows to love, honour and obey – only as mother and angel of the house, but also the fragrant bedmate, ever at the ready. I think she was prepared to play that game: she never rallied to the feminist battle cries, and poured scorn on Simone de Beauvoir for her hypocrisy in writing *The Second Sex* but then admitting that all she had ever really wanted was to possess the ghastly Jean-Paul Sartre. I sometimes think Ma would have been happy enough in a cave, under the good old order of man as hunter-gatherer, woman as nurturer.

Perhaps the collapse of their marriage can be seen as a portent of a broader cultural change which has spread through domestic life in Western society over the last half-century, fuelled by the liberalisation of the family and the laws which buttress it. What I have seen during this period is that as women have become more determined, articulate and effective, so men have become weaker, lazier and more confused and frightened by the challenge of living up to the potency that is implicitly expected of them. Yet at the same time both sexes cling to their Victorian stereotypes: trouser-wearing women continue to want to be seduced and even dominated by powerful men, while men expect women to flatter their vanity by accepting their authority and showing them respect. (On that particular score, not much has changed since the writing of that horrid play *The Taming of the Shrew*.)

Let me put it another way. I think men have become a bitter disappointment to women – not at all what their mothers had cracked them up to be and perhaps altogether an enfeebled breed whose moment at the top of the evolutionary tree has passed.

For all the talk of liberation and equality over the last 50 years, women seem to me to have continued to fantasise Emma Woodhouse's Mr Knightley as their beau ideal of manhood – someone fundamentally competent who remembers to pay the bills on time and is handy with a screwdriver, someone with a modicum of intelligence and sensitivity prepared to slap you round the face if you are being silly. But where are such creatures – males with a firm purchase on the steering wheel of life – to be found? Even Jane Austen knew that there weren't enough to go round. Drunks and liars abound, as do the hopelessly self-centred and emotionally hobbled, while the ones you can have fun with and talk to become increasingly likely to take sexual interest only in each other.

Anything more noble is hard to come by: and even the luckier women are left with a choice between steady but dull Robert Martin, fatuous Mr Elton, and slippery and amusing Frank Churchill, a fellow who would not have given the low-octane Jane Fairfax an altogether easy time, one feels.

My mother took a marital punt on a Frank Churchill. After that went belly-up, she found a Mr Knightley but was too demoralised to trust either him or herself. 'I always wanted a man who would love me to bits,' she said. But her guard was too high and her hide too tough to let John Sheneman do the business, so for the rest of her life – to borrow a phrase from Henry James – she was 'ground in the very mill of the conventional'. As for my father – well, I think he was frightened off because my mother saw through him and told him truths about himself that he didn't want to hear: specifically, that he had been a fool to follow so closely in his father's footsteps without the same pair of seven-league boots. My sympathy for him remains limited.

As I've already implied, my mother's last years were miserable, irradiated only by the love of my wonderful sister, and the support of her loyal friend Barbara. She was in constant dull pain as osteoporosis and arthritis withered her bone and muscle. Nothing gave her pleasure, though she put a brave grumpy face on things and kept hold of the tatters of her independence. I visited her in hospital for a week after she had had a futile operation to replace a broken hip. My sister and I thought that she might rally, but she was disinclined to contribute the necessary effort, sickened by the antibiotics and bracing talk of a lovely convalescent home in which she would not be allowed to cross her legs for three months. During my penultimate session at her bedside, she lay there vacantly and could barely be bothered to respond. At this stage of the game, there really was nothing more to say: she was signing off. Eventually, I pecked her cheek and made to leave. Turning to wave as I reached the door of the ward, we looked at each other for the last time: her expression was a mirthless grimace of mock-exasperation. Then she lifted one arm and dropped it on the bed – a curiously uncharacteristic gesture which seemed half blessing, half surrender.

Hours later she drifted into a sort of dozy coma and died gently at dawn with my sister and me at her side. The death certificate specified heart failure, septicaemia and bla-bla-bla but they might just as well have put 'accidie', sometimes spelt 'acedia' – the fatal sin of despair, common among medieval monks and nuns who dropped their rosaries, laughed at the mumbo-jumbo and slammed the door on the possibility of God's grace. Ma gave up on life, and who will blame her? I just wish she hadn't left it feeling so short-changed.

One cliché – no, one downright lie – peddled about the passing of someone you have loved is that you are bequeathed a consoling, calming sense that the soul is at peace and free of worldly care. This is not my experience, in which the dead hover anxiously. I am neither confidently religious nor naively superstitious, but I continually sense the unquiet presence of my mother's restless spirit, stalking me, watching me, waiting for me. I still worry about her. I suspect that she is holed up somewhere she doesn't much care for, bored and truculent. My dreams are haunted by her imminent return: she is always round the corner or in the next room or about to telephone, coming to get me.

So like most of us, I have travelled through life with a knapsack of unfinished business on my back: what fills it doesn't bear the crippling weight of remorse or vengeance, but it's uncomfortable and constricting all the same. The difference for me and those whose experience has been similar is that I can't unfasten the broken zip or find the key: what the knapsack does contain I have no way of telling. And even after writing this memoir – after trawling for facts and searching my heart – the enigma persists.

A wise woman to whom I recently related the heart of my story told me that I needed to stop looking for a solution, a resolution or even an explanation: life can't be catalogued into neatly labelled folders. 'Closure', that hideous cliché, is a delusion. Instead she counselled me: 'Reconcile yourself to your ambivalence.' I think she is right: and if I can't quite reconcile myself to an ambivalence that still seems to teeter in the balance, at least I can recognise it and finally move on.

Acknowledgements

I have drawn with gratitude and profit on the memories, reflections and knowledge of Drusilla Beyfus, Sue Bourne, Alastair Bruton, Frances Coady, Tony Delano, Sarah Duce, Fionna Espada, Mark Frith, Felicity Green, Patrick Griggs, Sharon Jallow, David Kynaston, Katy McPhee, Tony Miles, Mike Molloy, Caroline Moorehead, Val Newby, Felicity Rubinstein, Alison Wall and Christopher Ward.

Special thanks to Aurea Carpenter, Caroline Dawnay, Jane Haynes and Candia McWilliam, and above all, to my sister Anna Dempsey and partner Ellis Woodman.

Some minor names in the text have been changed.